WILD
BROTHER

WILD
BROTHER

BY

Ronald Rood

Drawings by Wendell Minor

TRIDENT PRESS
NEW YORK

500.9
R 776 w

SBN: 671–27059–1
LIBRARY OF CONGRESS CATALOG CARD NUMBER: 76–105868

PUBLISHED SIMULTANEOUSLY IN THE UNITED STATES AND CANADA
BY TRIDENT PRESS, A DIVISION OF SIMON & SCHUSTER, INC., 630
FIFTH AVENUE, NEW YORK, N.Y. 10020

PRINTED IN THE UNITED STATES OF AMERICA

ACKNOWLEDGMENTS

Grateful acknowledgment is made to the following publishers for permission to reprint previously published articles:

American Girl for "Nature's Rascals," July, 1965.

Audubon Magazine for "The Cicadas Are Here!" May-June, 1960; "Pokey—A Forest Fire Refugee," July-August, 1961; "Uncanny Cat," November-December, 1967; "Don't Count the Spreading Chestnut Out," March-April, 1968; "La Cucaracha," November-December, 1968. Copyright National Audubon Society.

Esquire Magazine for "Those Spring Peepers," "The Killer Whale," "A Half-Ton of Mermaid," and "The Terror of the Treetops." Copyright, ©, 1954, 1959, 1960, by Esquire, Inc.

Frontiers for "My Shoe-Button Lady," April, 1962.

Pageant Magazine for "The Mischievous Raccoon," May, 1968;

"The Ph.D. with Feathers," July, 1968.

The New York Times for "Living Things Adjust to Cold," "Plant Ballet," "Galls," "The Four-Footed Niblers," "Bluebird," "Sounds of September," "Wintertime Antics," and "Birds' Nests." Copyright, ©, 1965, 1966, 1967, 1968, by The New York Times Company.

Yankee for "Friendly as a Beartrap," September, 1966, and "The Tidal Waifs," July, 1967.

Vermont Life for "The Impatient Spring," reprinted by *The Reader's Digest*, copyright, ©, 1969; and for "Bullheads."

Vermonter for "Insects of Vermont," September, 1966, and "The Look of Christmas," December, 1966.

R.R.

Lincoln, Vermont
1969

Dedicated to our wild brothers who, though they have much to tell us, cannot speak for themselves.

Contents

CONTENTS

Introduction

WHEN THE American Indian roamed freely over his native land, he felt a sense of kinship with all around him. The bear, the trout, the owl—even the trees and the rivers— were to him his brothers. Didn't his legends tell of the spirit of the buffalo, the elk, the turtle who adopted human form and walked among men?

Thinking into the future, there was the chance that he too would someday change his earthly body for that of an eagle, perhaps, or a squirrel. A great chief might become a mountain or a cliff. And so he treated the world about him with respect, for it was peopled with many of his wild brothers.

In his dances and ceremonies he imitated the motions, the calls, the likenesses of these creatures who meant so much to him. He took upon himself their names and wove their stories into his folklore. Sometimes, as he drew aim on a deer or rabbit, he would breathe a quick prayer of apology to that animal's spirit. He'd explain soundlessly how he needed the meat for his family, the hide for clothing, the sinews for thongs. Then, having made his peace, he would send the arrow speeding toward its mark.

In many parts of the land he loved, the American Indian is no more. Many of his wild brothers, too, have passed on. But a few still remain. As their breech-clouted, moccasin-footed neighbor left them, he turned them over to his supposedly better-dressed and better-shod but often less appreciative cousin.

The day of kinship between man and nature, however, is not gone. It will never be gone as long as man needs to breathe the air, drink the water, muse at the antics of a squirrel, or stretch his mind and his body away from the fetters of civilization. What is gone is his awareness of this kinship.

And thereby lies the purpose of this book. Presented here in their natural surroundings are several dozen of these wild brothers. Luckily they have survived from those golden days. Since I have lived among them, I have gotten to know them as my brothers, too. Throughout the years I have found their lives to be sometimes serious, sometimes funny, sometimes without apparent sense to our dim understanding—but always fascinating. If their stories may lack interest at some point, the fault is not in their eventful lives, but rather in the telling. And if you find some thoughts repeated, it's because these stories represent some fifteen years of magazine articles—each unrelated to the others at the time it was written.

Here, then, are a few of my wild brothers. And yours, too.

SIGHTS
AND SOUNDS
OF THE SEASONS

Winter Whodunits

IT GETS mighty cold on these Vermont winter nights. So cold, in fact, that an antiquated neighbor of mine—eighty years old if he's a day—says he's only forty. Claims he's been frozen solid half his life.

However, there's a limit. And as I stood in the snow on our nature trail contemplating an abandoned thrush's nest, I figured the limit had been passed. Although the trees crack and pop with the cold at thirty below, even an unprotected bird's nest isn't supposed to shiver. Yet that's just what this nest was doing. It shivered so hard that a powder of snow fell off its domed roof and sifted down in the moonlight.

In fact, what was a deserted bird's nest doing with a roof anyway? Perhaps it wasn't as empty as I'd thought. As I was about to investigate, something on the ground caught my eye. There in front of me was a clue, or rather a whole series of them: tiny, lacy footprints. They ran in lines over the snow, etched in moonlight and shadow, and showing the drag mark of a long, slender tail. I was in the presence of a white-footed mouse, one of the many creatures who leave their stories in the snow.

A confirmed tree climber, the deer mouse, as it is often called, totes milkweed fuzz, feathers from a bird carcass, or even the stuffing from a mattress to remodel some bird's summer home. There it can be out of harm's way.

Like many other creatures, the deer mouse shows its

habits by its tracks. Its bounding gait, like an animated rubber ball, brings its hind feet in front of its forefeet so that the hind tracks register ahead of the smaller front ones. And like most tree dwellers, such as the squirrels, the tracks of its forefeet are paired with each other instead of being placed diagonally as are the tracks of rabbits and ground-dwelling field mice.

If you learn to identify a few tracks of the common animals you can be in on the start of a whole Winter Whodunit. Tracks and other signs speak volumes about the creature that made them. In fact, what we often call "the dead of winter" can be a fascinating time for animal study. Wherever a living creature goes it leaves a record.

Follow the white-foot, for instance. Here it disappears beneath a shelving ledge, leading you to its hidden storehouse of cherry pits or maple seeds. Here it has nipped and pulled at the frozen punkiness of a rotten log in hopes of finding a slumbering beetle. And over there it suddenly took a frenzied leap for the shelter of that evergreen, while the marks of wing feathers show where an owl had a near miss.

Not always are the signs easy to read, of course. Often you cannot even be sure you have a track at all. Sometimes the perfect hoofprint of a deer, say, leaves you puzzled because it's the only one of its kind in the unbroken snow. Hence the old saying among woodsmen: "If it's two or more, it's a track. If it's only one, it's an accident." And so your "hoofprint" turns out not to be that of a deer at all, but the mark where a piece of bark fell off and buried itself in the snow.

Speaking of deer tracks, the sharply pointed marks of those cloven hoofs are usually easy to spot. It is often possible to guess the sex of the animal, too. The prints of a doe tend to be sharper. This may be due not only to her delicate build but also to the way the buck paws the ground with his feet in autumn and early winter, wearing down his hoofs. In addition a buck may walk with toes pointed slightly outward.

Follow a deer in its wanderings and you may find where it

has browsed on the shrubbery. Lacking teeth in the front of its top jaw (deer, sheep, goats, cattle, and antelopes could all use a set of uppers), it has to twist buds and twigs from the stem instead of nipping them off. So you can tell the feeding activities of the deer by the frayed ends of the twigs. Rabbits, squirrels, and other creatures with buck teeth tilt the head sideways. Then they cut the twigs neatly on a slant, as if with a knife.

When you gaze at the trail of a deer, you may suddenly realize that it shows only half the number of tracks it should. The prints seem to be in single file, as if the deer were walking upright on its hind legs only. The explanation is that it steps in almost perfect register, with the hind feet falling into the prints just made by the front feet. Thus it leaves fewer tracks for an enemy to follow. It also makes less noise this way, for it takes less chance of stepping on a twig. Many wild animals walk in perfect register. Domestic dogs—and even cows and horses—are less fastidious and often show the prints of all four feet.

One of the best walkers is the fox. Its prints are usually in exact register, so that its trail through the snow looks like a single line of tracks about eight inches apart. A house cat's trail is like that of a fox, too, but with less space between the prints and, of course, with no sign of claw marks. A bobcat's tracks are similar to those of its domestic cousin, but larger.

For a fox, a winter's search for food must be an exercise in frustration. If the snow is right, you can often follow the trail of a fox through a whole series of disappointments. Here it sneaked up elaborately on a tuft of grass. You can see the flurry in the snow as it pounced, hoping to surprise a nest of meadow mice. False alarm.

In another place you can see the print of the fox's belly as it crouched low and inched forward, stalking a ground-feeding bird. Again the flurry in the snow and again the mouthful of nothing—if the lack of feathers or flecks of blood mean anything. And still another spot you can see where it blundered onto the resting place of a snowshoe hare but gave up the chase after floundering through the snow behind its rapidly departing derrière. The snowshoe hare, with its thick hairy footpads, can bound over the deepest drifts.

Then, finally, your fox forgets itself. It turns from a cunning predator into just a little dog as it disdainfully waters the scene of its latest failure. Obviously it didn't really care anyway. And almost as if to show it was on a diet all the time, it nonchalantly visits every bush and stub for a while, leaving its musky calling cards. If your dog is walking the same route with you, he dutifully follows along in the fox's trail, solemnly adding his own signature to the canine guest book.

Tracks, of course, are among the surest signs of the presence of your woodland neighbors. The flat-footed shuffle of a skunk or raccoon routed out of bed by a January thaw shows hind prints almost like the feet of a baby. The raccoon's front feet are like small hands, while those of the skunk leave more conventional paw marks. Snowshoe hares double up in running (hind feet first), as do cottontail rabbits. The great furry "snowshoes" of the former make dents in the snow sometimes eight feet apart at a bound.

Portly porcupines plow peacefully along making a double trail of prints. Hopelessly pigeontoed, as befits their habit of embracing the limbs of trees, they leave a channel in the snow like that of a rickety bulldozer. Beavers and muskrats waddle, too. Unlike the porky, their tails usually leave a mark: wide for the beaver, narrow for the muskrat. And, of course, neither one of them suddenly climbs a tree like the porcupine.

Unfortunately, tracks aren't always—or even usually—as clear as they appear in the scout manuals and camping books. More often they seem to be just a jumbled mess, especially if you're not in practice on this sort of thing. Besides, there are plenty of climbers and fliers that seldom leave bona fide "tracks" at all. So you have to look for other signs if you're interested in what's going on in the frosty winter-scape.

Tiny flecks, for instance, lying on the unbroken snow may each have the shape of a miniature fleur-de-lis. Looking up, you find they are the scales from the conelike catkins of a birch above you. Torn away and fluttering to the ground, the delicate scales show that a sparrow was looking for seeds, perhaps, or some other bird was searching for insects. In another spot a sifting of chaff beneath a tuft of last year's grass shows where a junco pulled the heads apart to get the seeds.

Out on the snow beneath the gaunt branches of a staghorn sumac is a fuzzy reddish mass. Here's where a bird, perhaps a chickadee, tried to satisfy the pinch of hunger in its tiny innards. Tearing the heads of the sumac apart, it searched for the slumbering spiders and insects that often take shelter there. Over here it whacked away at a goldenrod gall, drilling a hole in it like a pocket-sized woodpecker as it sought out the gall's inhabitant, a little white grub. And there it hopefully pecked at a frozen apple dried on the tree.

The snow is pulled and scraped away from a ledge at the steep side of a trail. This is the work of a deer, searching through the thinner snow cover on the slope for a few ferns or a bit of moss. If the snow has lain deep, you can probably see where the deer stood on its hind legs and reached as high as it could for buds and twigs. And if the deer are numerous, there may be a regular "browse line" through the forest where they've eaten everything they could among the lower branches. They may even chew on exposed clods of earth or gnaw the trunks of trees in an attempt to ease the pains of hunger.

Tree bark may find itself the unwilling object of attention from a number of winter wanderers. If it's nibbled way up on the limbs, this is probably the work of a porcupine. Porkies, however, don't confine their gnawing to tree limbs. They'll attack wood after it has been made into beams and boards, as woeful owners of tasty hunting camps can tell you. And a big old beech tree may be nibbled along the exposed roots and lower trunk only: The bark is too smooth for porkies to climb. In fact, about the only sizable animal that can go up a big beech is the black bear. You can sometimes find his claw marks in ascending crescents where he shinnied up the tree after beechnuts last fall before turning in for the winter.

Trees can tell you about other creatures, too. Mice and rabbits sometimes completely girdle a small tree by nibbling all the bark possible, the mice at the snow line and below, the rabbits as high as they can reach. Later, in spring, the height at which the rabbits have chewed will tell you how deep the snow was in winter.

A sapling bent and rubbed free of its bark is probably the work of last autumn's buck deer rubbing the "velvet" off its antlers. And a mouse or small bird impaled on a thorn marks the larder of a butcher-bird, or shrike. This is one of the few songbirds on earth that preys on others of its kind. I've watched a shrike chase a chickadee over a snowfield like a swallow after a moth—and with the same inevitable result.

The toed-in tracks of a ruffed grouse cross your trail among the evergreens. Placed one almost directly in front of the other, they weave under an overhanging branch. At another place they tightrope their way along a fallen log. The temporary "snowshoe" of comblike fringes along the toes makes them appear twice as large as they would be in summer.

Where the grouse has rested overnight in a spruce or has spent an hour nipping off the buds of a wild apple tree, scattered droppings in the snow beneath give evidence of the visit. And if you're lucky you may be able to see where the grouse dived into a snowbank to keep warm on a bitter night and then burst out again with the coming of day.

Bits of bark on the snow point out that a nuthatch has

poked into the crevices of a tree in its upside-down fashion. Thus the little bark-climbing bird cuts down on next summer's insect population before it can get started. Shreds of wood tell of a woodpecker's search for borers in a tree limb above. And a little heap of wedge-shaped scales on a stump show where a squirrel dined on a pine cone as he sat and watched for enemies.

The streams and ponds have their stories too. A stream-living beaver near my home apparently got a slow start on stocking his pantry for winter. Perhaps he'd been kicked out of his original home. Or he may have been dumped there by some disgruntled farmer who'd tired of all those engineering marvels near his farm pond and caught him in a box trap.

At any rate, the beaver got going too late to stow his food underwater and so he had to forage for himself all winter. To add to his troubles the stream was frozen too thickly to allow him to swim beneath the ice. So there he was, night after night, dragging home bits of aspen in pieces and plunging into the nearest patch of tumbling water. Then, unable to do a successful ferrying job through its icy shallows, he'd emerge again and hopefully try the next hole. I could see the evidence of his labors in drag-marks over the snow.

A mink bounds like a great furry inchworm along the edge of the stream. It leaves a trail of tracks two by two as it pops in and out of each hole, seeking trout, minnows, or crayfish. And once in two or three years I can see where an otter has visited a certain steep snowbank along a river near my home. Climbing to the top of the bank, it seems to ponder a moment. Then it lies down on its belly, tucks its forelegs along its side, and careens down its snow slide and out onto the ice.

A frozen stream is a fine place for tracks. All manner of creatures use it for a highway. The little river near our house keeps building stories in the snow nightly until a new snowfall comes along and wipes the slate clean.

Occasionally a warm winter's day will rouse a woodchuck

from his slumbers. Perhaps the meltwater from the snow seeps into his den and serves as a chilly alarm clock. Or maybe one of the skunks or rabbits, which often share his home, has blundered across his snoozing form. At any rate, once or twice during the winter he may awaken and stretch himself. Then, if he happens to come out on February 2, he fulfills the legend of Groundhog Day.

Tradition points to the woodchuck—or groundhog, if you prefer—as the only living creature stirring at this time of the year. But the big, nearsighted rodent should stay up a little longer. If his bleary eyes could only look beyond his shadow, he'd see that there's plenty going on, even now.

Impatient Spring

ORDINARILY OUR old maple tree is fairly well behaved. Of course it litters our front lawn with twigs and leaves after a heavy storm. Occasionally, too, it threatens our driveway when age becomes too much for one of its tottering limbs. On the whole, however, it's a stately, sedate old specimen. So I was quite unprepared on that February day when it hissed at me.

"Ps-s-s-t!" it said.

Puzzled, I stared at it. Now I could see that something was taking place. I had been conscious of half a dozen chickadees in the tree. However, they were behaving more like woodpeckers; they seemed bent on attacking a huge flake of bark on the trunk. As I watched, more of those strange hissing sounds came from the tree.

Carefully, for I wasn't dressed for wading in the snow, I made my way to the tree. And in the few feet from the driveway to the maple, I walked from winter into spring.

The part of the trunk that intrigued the chickadees was broadside to the rays of the morning sun. Although a thermometer in the shade was struggling to stay up in the teens, such was not the case with that slab of bark. Its dark color absorbed the sun's rays and, warmed by the heat from this little wooden stove, hundreds of cluster flies—bane of the fastidious housewife—stirred beneath the bark in their winter bed. Slightly larger than houseflies, they had hidden there last fall as newly formed adults, waiting for the spring mating season. Now, pushing and shoving, they made their way out into the sunshine. Every so often one would buzz its wings briefly. The loose bark, acting as a sounding board, magnified the noise: *ps-s-s-s-t!*

The chickadees, of course, were giving them a welcome. They pecked away at the emerging flies, enjoying this six-legged addition to their routine handout of suet and sunflower seeds. Now and again an ambitious fly would successfully run the gauntlet of stabbing beaks and escape into the air. It would be followed instantly by a chickadee, which snapped it up, nose-dived, and returned to the tree.

For nearly two hours the barkside banquet continued. Then the sun moved, abandoning the tree trunk to strike the thermometer, which soared to the mid-forties. With the coming of shade to cool their home, the flies slipped back into winter. And the chickadees returned to the bird-feeder.

Such little tastes of spring make it hard to say, really, when spring actually *does* begin. The calendar gives one date. The groundhog and his shadow foretell another. Countless little clues like a bunch of flies that cannot wait give still another.

One of the first spring flowers, for instance, may have already been waiting for those same buzzing flies. And "waiting" is just the word, for early spring insects may be vital to its existence. The flower is the peculiar purple-striped cup of the skunk cabbage, first cousin of the jack-in-the-pulpit and of the philodendron on your windowsill.

Sometime in late winter a hidden impulse triggers the skunk cabbage into life. Nothing can yet be seen aboveground, but the roots, buried a foot or more beneath the soil along a stream or marsh, begin to convert their stored food into energy. More energy is produced than can be used by the growing skunk cabbage bud: The excess is turned into heat. The heat builds up in this bootstrap operation until the bud lies in the dark in its own little incubator. Melting away the frost with temperatures approaching that of the human body, it forges its way upward.

Having risen aboveground, the skunk cabbage proceeds to demonstrate how it got its name—*Symplocarpus foetidus,* which is merely a scientific way of saying "the plant that smells." Little glands in the tissues produce a powerful odor, supposedly reminiscent of skunk, although to me it's more like a garbage heap. Wafted by the breeze, the odor calls to flies, restless beetles, and other insects wakened by the sun. Landing on the pollen-laden center beneath the plant's fleshy hood, they wander around, optimistically searching for the nonexistent trash pile, and in the process they fertilize the curious blossom. Thus it gets a running start on spring while less venturesome flowers are still underground.

The same moist ground that bears skunk cabbages may yield other spring hopefuls. Walk within a hundred feet of almost any brook or stream on a mild winter day. The chances are you may find a creature that insists on living its span backwards—climaxing its life in winter rather than in summer. Creeping over the snow, its slender dark body absorbing heat from the slanting sun, the winter stone fly is nearing the end of its existence. For months it has been a flattened nymph clinging to the bottom as it crawled about in the swift current and fed on other aquatic creatures. Depending on the particular species, it may have had an underwater life of a year or more. Now, instead of waiting for another warm summer, it pokes its way up through the grasses and debris at the river's edge. Although the half-inch creature has wings, it seldom uses them, but prefers to walk—or, if the sun gets hot enough, to run.

Clambering over the snow, it seeks out another of its kind. If it is successful it may mate, lay its eggs along the parent stream, and die before the ice has left its river.

The sun is a heat lamp to many creatures besides the stone fly. On a late winter walk you can find other early risers, if you look: spiders that creep over the surface of the snow as if in a dream, little brown caterpillars called from their grass-roots slumbers, wingless crane flies walking on their long legs over the honeycombed snow until you touch them. Then they collapse and fall down between the crystals. You may see gnats that fly in feeble circles until a cold draft hits them and they stall out. Brown miller moths work up enough energy to flit across an opening in the woods; the sugar-maker will call them "sap moths" when they get into his buckets a few weeks later.

You might even be treated to the improbable sight of a butterfly twinkling over the snow. The mourning cloak, decked in heat-absorbent brown, red, and blue, with cream-bordered wings, has stirred from its hollow tree. Now it flits to a broken maple twig and samples a drop of sap. As soon as the sun wanes, it goes back to its tree house.

As the days lengthen, more harbingers appear. The skunk, after a winter punctuated by periods of restlessness, finally decides to call it quits. It can't sleep any longer anyway, for the breeding season is fast approaching. Rousing from its underground den, it pokes around in search of venturesome insects, old apples uncovered by the retreating snow or—opportunist that it is—a member of the opposite sex. As it putters along it blunders into all kinds of hazards, from inexperienced dogs to irate chicken owners. Each blunder is announced on the breeze that flows past my house. However, such is the good-natured attitude with which the skunk greets life that it has probably forgotten the whole affair by the time I get the first sniff.

Gifted with much the same outlook, the raccoon also rouses itself to meet spring in advance. You can find its tracks, looking almost as if made by some pint-sized human walking barefoot and on all fours, in the snow. They're somewhat like the trail of the skunk, but the latter often humps along, slightly like a portly measuring worm. Hence skunk tracks may appear two by two instead of in the more rambling pattern made by the raccoon. Again like the skunk, the coon is not fussy about what it eats. Often the first hint you get that the ringtailed little burglar has awakened is the clatter of your garbage pail cover being knocked off in the dark.

Out in the woods the black bear yawns and stretches. Curled up beneath a ledge or a giant tree root, it has slept fitfully all winter, sustained by its thick layer of fat. Having stuffed its innards with pine needles and other debris, it seems to feel no need for food. Now, as much out of curiosity as anything else, it may rouse itself for a short walk. Then it returns for a few more weeks of slumber, like a man who wakens and resets the alarm clock for forty more winks.

Even the four-footed nibblers, especially the rabbits and deer, get a new lease on life. While the snow was deepest, it covered all of their food except what projected above the surface. Now as the snow settles, new twigs and buds are exposed daily. A walk in an old pasture or half-grown woodlot where young growth is dense will show the fresh marks of the rabbits. The ends of twigs are cut on a slant, for rabbits have to tilt their heads to slice with those buck teeth. The deer, having no uppers in front, must twist their food from the branch, leaving the twigs frayed and splintered.

For the twigs themselves this must represent a sort of double jeopardy. They're exposed the first time in early winter before the snow deepens. Then after it has protected them so well, the snow melts down and leaves them standing there, inviting a passing nip or two as they become available once again.

Of course the mice have been busy at ground level as well. When the snow was heavy, the tracks of a mouse looked merely like a double trail of tiny footprints here and there, emerging from a mouse-sized hole in the snow and burrowing down again. Now the whole traffic pattern of the little rodent is shown: a maze of trails made by tireless small feet. Packed down, these trails stay longer than the softer snow around them. Sometimes they lace the entire landscape, for as many as two hundred mice may populate a single acre of ground.

The first stirrings of spring have a sound of their own, too. Since it is the brink of a new time for seeking a mate, such an important occasion deserves to be announced. As early as February the quiet of my snowy woods may be shattered by the drumming of a woodpecker. This feathered riveter can speak in little more than a squawk, so he advertises his availability in a different manner: Finding a hollow tree stub, or even a projecting piece of bark that has just the right resonance, he whacks away. Sometimes I wonder what the reaction must be among the insect population beneath the bark when that din erupts over their heads.

Then too, there's the spring song of the chickadee. All fall and early winter the black-and-white waif has said his name over and over as he searched every crack for insects or hammered away at goldenrod galls for the grub that each contains. Now, apparently energized even more by the lengthening days, his boundless vitality bursts out in a new song. It's a high, sweet, two-note whistle. You can copy it almost exactly by whistling the highest note your lips can form for one second. Then drop down two tones and whistle again for one second. Even to the uninitiated, the chickadee's message is as clear as the words it seems to say: "Spring . . . soon."

People hearing it at first sometimes think it's the call of the phoebe. However, this bird doesn't arrive until April. Besides, its note is almost spoken—a positive "fee-bee"—not a clear whistle.

No doubt every bit as meaningful to the ears for which they are intended are the courtship calls of other creatures: the moonlight yip of the red fox, the unearthly yowl of the bobcat, the first thumpings of the rabbit as it drums with its hind feet to announce to prospective mates that the time has nearly come to start living up to their reputation.

Sometimes the sounds of spring penetrate even the most

well-ordered existence. "Wish you could get over here to listen to this crazy thing," Dana Haskin of Waitsfield told me over the telephone one evening in mid-March. "It goes beep-beep-beep about a hundred times a minute out in a grove of hemlocks. A bunch of us thought it might be some kind of electronic gadget that had come to earth in a parachute. It was loud enough to be heard by a friend through her double glass windows. But when we went out with flashlights to find it, it took off and lit in another tree. And no parachute would do a thing like that."

We finally decided that it was just another sign of the season—the mechanical wolf whistle of the tiny saw-whet owl. This personable elf, barely larger than a robin, nests early, like most of the owls, while humans are still shivering and wondering if winter will ever let up. Owl babies, however, have downy coats of winter underwear to help them stand the cold.

Spring can make itself known even while you're shoveling your walk for the tenth time. Early last winter the predominant color scheme was black-on-white as the bare branches stood out against the snow. Now, suddenly, you realize the colors have softened. The black is not as black. It may have a reddish tinge if you're looking over a valley wooded with maples, a chocolate color with alders, or a yellowish hue where the willows are present.

Individual trees and shrubs are changing color, too. With each little thaw, each lengthening day, new life seeps into countless twigs. Their buds swell to half again their original size, even though they remain tightly shut. The elms growing along the river and hanging over the snowy streets seem to be strung with rusty beads as each bud stands out in silhouette.

If the black isn't as black as it used to be, the white isn't as white, either. Of course much of this is due to the accumulation of the dirt and debris of the winter months. However, it may also be caused by a creature known as the snow flea.

This odd insect is about the size and color of a speck of pepper. It acts about as a speck of pepper might, too, if that spicy condiment should come to life. Cocked beneath the abdomen of the snow flea is a taut little spring, bent double and held in place by a trigger. When the trigger is released, the tiny insect is catapulted into the air. Hence another common name, "springtail."

Of course an individual snow flea would not be noticed in all that whiteness. But this wingless creature with the built-in pogo stick doesn't do things individually. On a moderate day in late winter an entire lawn or hillside may be made gray as snow fleas come to the surface in myriads to soak up the sunshine. I've walked up a woodland path during a February thaw and come back along the trail an hour later; each of my footprints in the snow was carpeted by thousands of the tiny creatures. Possibly the compressed snow allowed more light to seep down below, calling them up for a spring frolic.

Although nobody seems to have counted them, springtails must be among the most numerous of all the insects. They can find a living almost anywhere, feeding on algae, lichen, and plant debris. As Mrs. Eleanor Ellis of Springfield wrote to me: "I'm glad they're harmless or I'd pity every poor stray dog that comes through our yard!"

There are dozens—hundreds—of other little signs telling us that, even while it looks as if we're in another ice age, winter is really being pushed aside by spring. Of course there's the dandelion that chances to blossom on the sunny side of a lawn next to a building in January or the pussy willow that suffers a whopping case of insomnia and blooms from Thanksgiving to Mother's Day. Things like these get their names in the paper. But the countless little hints of the burgeoning season are there, too, for the looking.

And, much as I love to see the first robin and hear his hopeful chirp in the same old sugar maple that sheltered those cluster flies, there's one thing sure: Even though he may be here to get the first worm that dares poke up through the matted grass under that tree, the robin is really no early bird at all.

Wintertime Antics

LEGEND POINTS to the groundhog as if he were the only living creature to stir in winter. If the big, waddling rodent doesn't see his shadow on February 2, spring will be early and, the legend continues, the creature will stay aboveground the rest of winter. If he does stay, he will find plenty of stirring animals to keep him company.

When that old sparrow's nest rustles and shakes in the still winter air, stop for a closer look. Although supposedly long since abandoned, a touch might reveal the large eyes and bewhiskered face of its present occupant: a white-footed mouse.

These tawny creatures often remodel an old nest for their own use, roofing it over and lining it with soft material. Investigate a likely looking nest in the yard or tap on a birdhouse. The sudden appearance of a startled face might mean new neighbors.

That forlorn winter sun has yet enough energy to bring warmth, even if the temperature is well below freezing. The surface of the snow, on any but the bitterest day, may become a veritable little zoo. Dark-bodied caterpillars, defying the cold, crawl slowly along. Spiders, wingless crane flies, soldier beetles, and spindly gnats creep over the frozen surface as if in a dream. Even a few small dusky moths or the "winter butterfly" (mourning cloak) may cruise about for an hour or two.

The secret lies in the capacity of dark colors to soak up the sun's warming rays. Just as a black patch of asphalt will melt the snow around itself, so the dark bodies of insects and spiders become heated. The penetrating warmth calls them out of hiding and they meander over the snow. We once collected nearly three dozen insect species on a single snow-covered meadow.

The snow also records other activities. Every animal track tells a new tale. Even bits of plant material have their story. Tiny flecks, shaped like a fleur-de-lis, are probably scales from the catkins of a neighboring birch, torn apart by some finch, redpoll, sparrow, or other seed-eating bird. A little pile of wedge-shaped scales shows where a squirrel sat and dined on a pine cone.

Your ears, too, tell you winter is not dead. On a mild day that little frog, the spring peeper, may wake from his slumbers in the leaf mold and pipe a few hopeful notes at the winter sun.

There are birdsongs in the air, too. The high "spring soon" note of the chickadee tells what will shortly happen to that black-capped bird's fancy. Attract him by imitating his call: Whistle a single high note for two seconds; drop down two tones and whistle a second note.

Woodpeckers, lacking suitable voices to charm the ladies, now make their calls by drumming on a hollow stump. Such an outburst would be unthinkable in December. One exuberant fellow used to whack away early each morning at the eaves troughs near our window. He made a fine alarm clock.

This is the time, too, to listen for owls for it is their courtship season. Silent much of the year, they may now be as vocal as a cat on a fence. Owls nest earlier than most birds, often before the last snow has fallen. Each species has its own peculiar call, from the great horned owl's measured hoot to the quavery, descending whistle of the screech owl.

City dwellers can be on the lookout for these birds, too. One winter I saw a snowy owl on the superstructure of New

31

York City's Triboro Bridge. Last winter one took up residence in a steeple in Burlington, Vermont. There it sat like a carved statue, surveying the traffic below and causing a panic among the pigeons and starlings.

So, even as dry weeds whip in the wind and tree trunks crack with the cold of nature's icebox, life simmers on in countless little animal stoves.

Living Things Adjust to Cold

WHAT CREATURE dons a suit of underwear for winter? Which one installs a heating plant? What living things make use of a heat-producing color scheme? Many plants and animals must adjust to cold weather in some way. A walk through nearby gardens and parks will reveal a number of species who have successfully mastered the challenge of winter.

The "underwear set" includes several of our most common winter residents, the birds. In winter, their feathers are in two layers. There is a windproof cloak of outer "contour" feathers which gives characteristic shape and color and a hidden layer beneath of downy under-feathers which traps and holds the warm air generated by the body.

There is great insulation value to this double layer. On a tiny bird, such as a sparrow or chickadee, the total thickness of these feathers is scarcely a quarter of an inch. Yet in that space the temperature ranges from far below zero on the coldest days to perhaps 105 degrees near the body.

The ruffed grouse or "partridge" of our rural areas has even refined this almost perfect heat trap. Most of the winter contour feathers of a grouse have a downy little sprout at their base for added insulation. The feathers extend down the shins in winter like fluffy ski pants. Then there's the added fillip of scaly fringe which develops along each toe:

"snowshoes" to keep the birds from sinking into drifts.

While winter birds meet the weather head-on with cold-weather jackets, the heating-plant approach satisfies the needs of the honeybee. In cold weather, the bees cluster in a loose mass within the hive. By exercising their wings and legs, they keep the temperature of the hive well above the freezing point. The living core of the mass may be at a temperature of 50 degrees or more. As the bees on the outside cool off, they burrow in toward the center. Sometimes, by putting an ear against the hive, you can hear the faint hum of this living furnace.

Like the hotel lobby which in winter may fill up with people who have merely come in to get out of the cold, the warm beehive also attracts visitors. A mouse or two may move in during an unguarded moment and, in the course of time, there may be a few mouselets as well sharing the warmth (and the honey) until they're evicted.

Central heating works for other insects, too. Under a loose board or stone may be found thousands of ladybird beetles huddled together. In an attic or warehouse may be more thousands of cluster flies, packed several layers deep. The life processes of these myriads of tiny bodies, each breathing and slowly keeping alive the spark of life, adds a few degrees of warmth to the surroundings.

Outside, along city streets and country roads, wind and snow slash at the trees. Take a twig indoors and examine it with a magnifying glass. With soil frozen in its top layers, the tree is hard put to get a supply of water in winter. It must conserve what it has. Each bud is covered with a waxy, varnishy, or felted layer. Against these protective layers, the drying gales of winter have little effect.

On the inside of a large horse chestnut bud is still another protection. Underneath the resinous bud-scales is a cottony layer of cellulose. It wraps the delicate tip like a white blanket, tempering the winter cold.

Many have probably observed rhododendrons in very cold

weather. The leaves curl inward and hang down as if they were huddled against the cold. This phenomenon appears when the temperature drops well below freezing. Evidently the water within the leaf cells is translocated in response to the cold temperatures. If curled rhododendron leaves are taken into warm temperatures, they will unfold and assume their normal position.

Resinous shellac covers the eggs of the tent caterpillar, closely wrapped around a bare apple twig. Gypsy moth eggs rest on a tree trunk, imbedded in a mat of hairs from the mother's body. Praying mantis eggs winter safely in a cradle made of hardened foam spun by the female. Most likely she produced the eggs a few days before her body dropped lifeless to the ground. Spider eggs repose on a mattress of silk beneath the bark of a tree. Moth cocoons lie wrapped in a dead leaf. Cut open a gall on the stem of a rosebush or last autumn's goldenrod. Inside may be the gall's summer inhabitant, a portly grub perhaps, battened down for the winter.

In Vermont, there's still another way one creature beats winter cold. Many Vermonters will tell of it without batting an eye. It seems that one of the East's chilliest lakes is Memphremagog, on the Canadian border. A visitor to this northern section of Vermont is liable to be greeted by a sign that says, "Welcome to Memphremagog—Home of the Fur-bearing Trout." Such a critter, however, although the lake is perfectly fresh, had better be taken with a grain of salt.

CREATURES
OF THE LAND

The Mischievous Raccoon

WHEN the dear old lady came to call, Peg gave me a rueful glance. Now we were in for it. Once the lady started to talk, it would be half an hour before she even paused for breath.

But we needn't have worried. Ten minutes after she had arrived and was just warming up to an analysis of the town's birth rate, she stopped. Mouth open, she stared at the kitchen ceiling. A small black hand reached down, felt around, and vanished.

We saw the hand, too. I was about to say something, but Peg beat me to it. "Raccoon. Excuse me," my wife said, as if this explained everything. Then, with a wicked gleam in her eye, she fled, abandoning me to our flabbergasted neighbor.

Smiling politely, I explained the apparition. The black hand, I told my guest, belonged to some ten pounds of inquisitive lady raccoon who went by the name of Scamper. A Vermonter in a neighboring village had discovered her when she was a tiny waif on a trellis just out of reach of a couple of marauding dogs.

Nobody knew where the mother was so the homeowner telephoned to have me pick up the little creature. As one who is interested in wildlife and who has an abandoned farm on which animals can roam, I often get such calls.

Scamper took to the whole idea at once and soon became a part of the family. She went everywhere with us and made it her duty to inspect everything, from the innards of the family washing machine to the light fixture I was currently putting in the ceiling.

My wife, to her credit, didn't desert me in my hour of trial with the dear old lady. When Peg figured I'd suffered long enough, she called me upstairs to help with the raccoon. Our loquacious neighbor, figuring we had our hands full, promised to finish her story some other time.

Actually, all this was most unusual for a raccoon. Not the exploring hand, of course, for a raccoon is built of question marks from black nose to bushy tail. The unusual aspect was that the raccoon put a stop to a conversation. The more usual thing is for a raccoon to be the best conversation piece on four legs.

In fact, with a raccoon in the family, you don't have to worry about saying a thing. All you have to do is watch. As a child, I once had a toy tractor that could not be shut off. Once it was wound up, it continued until it ran down. A raccoon is like that except that it seldom runs down. At least that's the way it's been with the seven coons we've had.

The black-masked little creature gets just as wound up in the wild, too. Everything's worth at least a brief investigation. A raccoon puttering along may turn over a pebble here, a piece of bark there. It gives a stinkbug an experimental nip and thrusts a hopeful arm down a mousehole. And half the time it's doing this, it's talking to itself with little grunts, churrs, sniffs, and chuckles. An area worked over by a raccoon in its search for grubs, fruit, mushrooms—in fact, nearly anything edible—often looks as if a small war had taken place there.

I first learned about coon curiosity before we had any raccoons of our own. One day during my boyhood, when I was sitting quietly on the bank of a little pond fishing, a noise in the grass attracted my attention. A raccoon had somehow surprised a pond turtle and had managed to get it up on the bank. Now it batted the unhappy creature along with its front paws to an opening in the grass where it could work on it. For nearly an hour, while I watched, that raccoon tried to solve the puzzle of a turtle in the shell. Turning the turtle over and over, the raccoon poked and gnawed. It tried to get down and look at the turtle from underneath, all to no avail.

The turtle, of course, was hardly flattered by all this attention. Finally it had had enough. Seizing its chance, it nipped one of those little black fingers and quite literally set the raccoon back on its heels. Then, followed closely by a sharp little black nose and drummed out of the vicinity by an indignant churring, the turtle made its way back to the water with all possible speed.

Raccoons are very careful about those almost-human front paws. What a nose is to a bloodhound or an eye to an eagle, those hands are to a raccoon. They are like a pair of antennae tipped with five fingers and no thumb. Although they are constantly exploring, the hands are quickly jerked away if they touch something that snaps, buzzes, or bites.

A raccoon's hands seem almost to have a will of their own, poking and prying, feeling and sorting, while their owner gazes absently about with nearsighted black eyes and samples the night sounds with rounded teddy bear ears. In fact, after watching our own raccoons paw through the mud at the edge of a pond, I have almost come to believe that the hands are gifted with as keen a sense of taste as that of feel. They sort through all the goo with a patting, washing motion and come up again and again with a snail, a tadpole, an edible tuber. How they can find such delicacies in all that debris is a mystery—unless, as I say, raccoons have taste buds in their hands.

All this sloshing at the raccoon's habitat—the edge of a stream or pond—has led to the belief that it has to wash its food before it eats. In fact, its scientific name, *Procyon lotor*, freely translated means "the little dog who washes." But, apparently, it's more like Junior playing with his baby cereal in the high chair; it just feels nice. This, perhaps, explains the absorbing spectacle of a raccoon washing a fish.

Scamper—or Hezekiah or Lollipop or any of our four other coons—would give most daily food a good dunking if water was near. They'll carry it about twenty feet to douse it in the drinking dish. Any farther than that, however, doesn't seem to be worth the effort. And they'll eat their dog biscuits and fig bars unwashed. We had to be careful about this food dunking when we gave them raw hamburger. Otherwise, after a little vigorous washing, there'd be no more hamburger. Only a puzzled raccoon.

Life gets officially under way for "the black masked little bear," as the Indians used to call the raccoon, sometime in late winter. All over its range, from Atlantic to Pacific, southern Canada to Central America, the raccoon tribe undergoes some sort of giant, individualized family reunion. Normally quite solitary on the few acres of overgrown wasteland or swamp that it calls home, the raccoon now ranges much wider in search of companionship.

Since females as well as males may wander in late February, March, and April, this can lead to complications. Two or three males may come upon a female at the same time. Or she may wander into an erstwhile friendly conclave of highly eligible bachelors and precipitate a free-for-all.

A fighting raccoon is well-nigh invincible. Ears laid back against its head, white fangs bared, it bristles to half again its size. Crouching so low that an enemy has to expose its own underbelly in order to attack, it snarls and hisses its defiance. If the attack does come, the raccoon is such a mass of squirming muscle and thick, loose fur that, even if the enemy gets a grip, the raccoon turns in its skin and slashes deep with teeth or claws.

Two raccoons in battle, however, come out surprisingly well. There's a snarling, snapping whirlwind of gray-brown fur that moves so fast you cannot even tell what kind of animals are fighting. However, each is so agile and so well padded that the vanquished loses little more than his pride and the victor gains little more than a few mouthfuls of fur —plus, of course, the hand of the little lady who started it all. She, naturally, acts as if she couldn't care less while the argument is going on. However, she's been known to start a rousing fight of her own if a second female blunders onto the scene.

Once things have been ironed out, male and female travel together for a while. However, it's not long before the male (1) regrets his loss of bachelorhood or (2) becomes interested in another lady raccoon. He wanders off, in typical independent raccoon fashion, whenever the mood strikes him. This apparently is all right with his spouse, who hardly glances up from dousing an unfortunate frog.

Sometime in May or June her hollow tree receives a new set of boarders—three or four mewing, churring little raccoons. They're almost as naked, blind, and helpless as newborn kittens. They are about the size of kittens, too, with stubby tails giving little hint of the bushy fur with four or five rings that will grace them later. Their little faces with tightly shut eyes are crossed by a faint dark band ingrained right in the skin.

In about ten days the eyes of the cubs begin to open. Blue and bleary, they can pick out little more than the entrance hole of their tree house, darkened occasionally as their mother departs in the evening or returns in the morning. But as the cubs grow stronger, that raccoon curiosity asserts itself. They climb up to the hole with needle-sharp little claws.

Now they are faced with a problem: whether to remain in the safety of the familiar hollow tree or to explore the new world that beckons. Of course, since they are raccoons, the answer is obvious. By the time they are a month or six weeks old, they're beginning to crawl around on their tree. They look petrified with fear even as they take that next step, clinging spread-eagled with all four feet and advancing cautiously as if they'd never learn. But raccoons are expert climbers and before long they're playing tag around the tree like plump little squirrels.

It's often at this point that a nest of raccoons is discovered by some farmer or logger. My father used to tap or scratch on an old hollow tree if he was going to cut it down. One day I saw why he did this: In answer to his scratching, four little black-masked faces came to the entrance of a large hole twenty feet above our heads. My father left the tree untouched until the coons had moved.

When taken very young, raccoons make wonderfully clever pets. One day a man called up to tell me about two raccoons he'd found while he was cutting firewood. "The tree split open when it fell," he said, "and one of the babies was killed. The other two are all right, but their eyes are still closed and they'll probably starve."

I assured him the mother would come and take them to a new home, but he called me up again the next morning. "Their mother never came back. I heard them chattering and crying before I was within a hundred feet of the place," he said. "You could tell by their wailing that they hadn't had a thing to eat. When I felt them, they were as cold as ice. So I wrapped them in my jacket and brought them home after work."

We told him about the formula we'd used on Scamper and her relatives: a cup of milk, a teaspoon of honey, a dash of salt, and a medicine dropper. Plus a heating pad to keep their shivering little bodies warm. It worked wonderfully; the man had those raccoons for a couple of months until they got to be too frisky. Then, naturally, he gave them to me.

A pet raccoon is not an unmixed blessing. Hold one in your arms and you become the object of a major exploration. Those restless little hands feel of your wristwatch, your ring, your eyeglasses. They even poke down your collar and into your ear. Clench your fist loosely and they'll feel around inside it, too. They'll try to twist off every button. A teen-age girl who picked up Hezekiah one time at our home lost half her haircurlers before she could put him down.

In the tradition of that toy tractor I had as a child, a pet raccoon would keep going almost indefinitely. My logger friend had named his raccoons Peggy and Ronald for my wife and me; they nearly drove their namesakes wild during the next few months when we had them. As it's against the law to cage or restrain a wild animal, we merely allowed them the run of our Vermont farmyard. This was all right until they'd manage to sneak into the house. Then they'd be in the wastebasket, up on the table, into my window garden. When Peg opened the refrigerator, she had to be careful about closing it again; probably there'd be a small grizzled-brown animal sampling the food on the lower shelves while she moved the food around on the upper ones. In fact, we admitted that it was a relief when the terrible twosome struck off on their own.

They didn't forget us, however. Every few days, in winter, between fitful sleeps under an abandoned barn in the vicinity, they'd wade through the snow to our back door for a handout of cold cereal and canned dog food. But when the romantic spell of a February thaw took hold, they disappeared.

Under more normal circumstances in the life of the raccoon, the mother coon bears the brunt of her offsprings' playfulness. As the young ones widen their horizon beyond the hollow tree, they tumble after her on her nightly forays. Few sights are more appealing than four black-masked babies running along after their mother—sniffing where she sniffs, poking where she pokes, and sometimes going off on tiny side trips of their own.

If they come to the home of a ground-nesting bird, they reduce the eggs to a sticky mess, while the frantic parent bird flutters around them helplessly. Never far from water, young raccoons learn to feel in the stones and mud for frogs and crayfish. A patch of raspberries becomes a disaster area and every mud puddle is felt over minutely before the family moves on. They leave behind a maze of tracks made by those almost human "hands" and feet.

Nothing, however, compares to the exuberance of a family of raccoons in a cornfield. Although few of our pet raccoons seem to have liked raw corn, the tasty ears are irresistible to the little burglars in the wild. They like it just when the corn is at its milky best.

Seizing an ear of corn, a black-masked marauder pulls it down and tears away the husk. No sooner has it taken a bite, however, than it spies another ear on another stalk, tantalizingly unopened. So it takes a quick sample of this second ear. Then a third—and so on through the night. Multiply this by a family of four and you have an impressive husking bee.

So it goes through most of the summer. The raccoons travel along like a company of clowns, tugging and squabbling over every bit of food in backyards, swampy wasteland, and even suburban parks. Often one final rough-and-tumble that degenerates into a family argument sends them all packing in separate directions.

With the coming of winter each raccoon retires to a den beneath a ledge or in a hollow log. There it sleeps most of the winter, waking now and then to poke around for a few hours, then goes back to sleep. Slowly it uses up the layer of fat it has acquired at the expense of hundreds of insects, bird eggs, berries, earthworms, and offerings from an occasional garbage pail.

A raccoon, of course, is bedlam around a garbage pail. It hauls everything out, spreads it around, sometimes sits down with a jelly jar between its paws while it licks it out. After it's through the area looks as if it had been the scene of a beach party.

A friend of mine had a trash can behind his house which was visited frequently by an old "dog coon," as the males are often called. The raccoon would push the lid off the can and spend half the night inside, tossing out what it didn't want and consuming the rest.

"I got tired of cleaning up the mess in the morning," my friend recalled, "so I decided to fix that raccoon for good. My son and I found a huge rock and set it on top of the can. We knew he'd never get the cover off."

He paused so significantly that I had to ask the question. "But he took the cover off?"

"He took the cover off. Things were a worse mess than ever in the morning. So we sat up the next night to see what kind of superstrength he had, anyway."

He paused again, as if straightening out in his mind what he had seen. "How did he do it? Simple, of course, for a raccoon. He just stood up against the trash can—and rocked it until the stone fell off."

Overturned garbage, plundered cornfields, and the howls of irate chicken farmers who find their eggs and birds in a riot after Ringtail's visit have spelled the doom of many a coon. Seldom does he survive the ten or a dozen years he's been known to live in captivity. Though he has few natural enemies able to do him in, he continuously runs afoul of man. Raccoon hunts, complete with carefully bred coon hounds, have been a favorite moonlight diversion for more than two centuries in America.

Many a camper has discovered that if curiosity is the raccoon's number one characteristic, cleverness is right behind it. The two traits make for a winning combination. A coon can unstrap a lunch pail or unzip a zipper almost as well as you can. Twelve girl scouts on an overnight hike near my home found that their supposedly raccoon-proof wooden grocery box had been raided overnight. The butter and sugar and eggs were still almost all there—but mixed.

Raccoon meat is delicious, I'm told, though I'd feel guilty if I ever ate any. Raccoon caps and coats have long been a part of America. Mountain lions and wolves are seldom seen now, but almost any camper or vacationist in America still has a good chance of seeing a raccoon. So the playful little bandits have their redeeming features.

Scientists say the forebears of the raccoon may have trod the earth in that flat-footed amble some ten million years ago. A number of experimental models in the coon family have become extinct, but today the kinkajou and coatimundi of the New World, plus the giant panda of the Old World, still remain. And so does the raccoon, who somehow survives to raid your strawberry patch or wave a playful hand through a hole in the ceiling at a hastily departing visitor.

That little escapade, by the way, had its sequel. Scamper must have decided that the time had come to show that she, too, was an individual. For before she advertised her presence up over the kitchen by beckoning to us below, she thoughtfully nibbled the insulation off ten feet of brand-new wire.

Pokey—A Forest Fire Refugee

HE CAME running to us after he had lost his mother in a forest fire. We didn't want to have anything to do with him. We could see hundreds of sharp little needles underneath his black fur. But the ashes of the fire were still smoking and he cried aloud as his scorched feet made little puffs of dust.

Warner Pierce, a neighbor boy, scooped him up with a shovel. At once the little porcupine balled up into a silent mass of prickers. My son Tom pulled off his cloth jacket and held it like a net while Warner dumped the baby into it. Then, wadding it loosely, we carried the tiny orphan to the car.

"Well," Tom said as we unwrapped the bundle on the back seat, "what on earth are we going to do with him?"

We've spent more than a year searching for the answer to that question and we haven't really found it yet.

The first thing, however, was to get some food into the little fellow. We recalled seeing beech and fir trees de-barked by porcupines, so we gathered some of the branches. But the little quill-pig was too frightened to eat. All that day and evening he just huddled in the corner of a box.

When he still hadn't eaten the next morning, we decided to give him the universal food welcomed by all mammal babies—warm milk. I put on a heavy leather jacket and gloves and picked him up.

Holding him on his back, I poked at his mouth with a

49

medicine dropper. His long curved black claws were drawn together as a shield over his dark little nose. His black eyes were tightly shut. Plainly he expected this to be his last moment on earth.

But the instant I touched his lips with the sweetened milk, his resistance collapsed. Opening his eyes, he seized the dropper and pulled at it until the milk was gone. Then a pink tongue appeared for a moment and licked his lips.

That warm milk did wonders for his attitude toward life. His pincushion armor relaxed until he became astonishingly small, no larger than your doubled fist. In less than an hour he was exploring the kitchen floor. In two days he was so tame that I put away my leather jacket. He has never bristled at any of us since.

"What'll we call him?" asked Tom.

I had been reading Thornton Burgess stories to Roger as a bedtime treat. We had met Blacky the Crow, Peter Rabbit, Jimmy Skunk, and Prickly Porky. "Porky," suggested Roger. "But it's too bad he isn't a little bear cub. Then we could call him Smokey, like the bear who lost his mother in a fire."

"How about combining the two," asked Janice, "and making it 'Pokey'?"

Nobody knew then how fast or slow he could run. But after seeing him at top speed, we decided that Pokey was a good name all around. His gallop might get him a mile in a couple of hours. But it lasts only ten or twelve feet at a stretch. The rest of the time he noses along at his customary amble, which is about a third as fast as a man's leisurely walk.

From the first, he jumped at every sound. Although his ears are so short that they're hidden in the fur of his round head, they're surprisingly keen. Probably they make up for eyesight that lets him see only three or four feet ahead. While I was feeding him one evening, my wife Peg was mending in the next room. Pokey was murmuring contentedly as he downed his rations. Then Peg dropped a button on the floor. At the sharp sound, his quills came to full alert. He half-whirled to meet his unseen enemy. Even in the warm kitchen, with the soothing taste of sweetened milk, he couldn't forget that he was a wild creature.

"How does a porcupine play?" Janice asked one evening as she was doing a high-school report on our pet. "Does he chase his tail like a kitten?"

This tickled Roger. "Think what'd happen if he ever *caught* it!"

A few days later Janice's question was answered. Alison had just finished feeding Pokey in the kitchen. Suddenly she cried out in alarm. "Mother! Daddy! Come quick!"

When we got to the kitchen, she was standing in a corner. "Something's the matter with Pokey!"

He was doing a war dance. That's the only way you could describe it. With his back in an exaggerated arch like that of a cat on the Halloween designs, every quill raised, he whirled as if on a pivot. Four or five turns one way, four or five the other. Then straight backwards, at a run, bristle-tail swinging like a scythe. A couple of sideways hops, stiff-legged, then back into the spin again.

Around the kitchen he went. Every time he slowed down, we'd stamp our feet and start him up again. I've never seen a porcupine in full action against an enemy but this must have been Pokey's way of rehearsal. After watching him we decided there's only one thing as prickly as an angry porcupine. And that's a playful one.

One day Peg took Pokey to a teachers' meeting. Little ham actor that he is, he obligingly went through his spin for the delighted audience. But the best was yet to come. When they all sang "America" as part of their closing exercise, Pokey sat up and put his paws against his ears. All through the song he swayed from side to side and squinted his eyes in pain.

The last verse collapsed in pandemonium.

By the time he was two months old, he had graduated to cereal, crackers, green leaves, and potato chips. Our baby was growing up—in more ways than one. This was evident one night when Peg woke me. "Ps-s-st!" she whispered. "What's that?"

We listened in the dark. Scrape, scrape. Then a pause. Scrape, scrape again.

"Mice," I suggested hopefully.

Peg snorted. "That's no mouse. That's a porcupine. And ten to one he's helping himself to our furniture."

When we got downstairs and flipped the light switch, Pokey blinked pleasantly at us from the top of the kitchen table. He'd tipped the butter over and helped himself. He'd taken several gouges out of a bowl of apples. Now he was nibbling at the table edge— tablecloth and all—as if it were an ear of corn. Squealing with pleasure, he ran across the table to greet us.

The next morning we asked the children what should be done with him.

"We can't let him go in the woods," Alison protested. "He'd walk up to the first hunter he saw."

"Besides," Tom added, "he's not even afraid of dogs. He wouldn't know how to protect himself."

It was probably true. Pokey got along fine with Jack, our big shepherd dog. He kept those murderous daggers covered as they played together. He loved to crawl up Jack's heavy fur and ride on his back. I could imagine just how long he'd last if he met a hound in the woods. By the time he found out the dog's intentions, it would be too late.

I helpfully suggested putting him in a zoo. They looked at me, shocked. Put our own porcupine in a common zoo?

So I got some wire and made him a cage. But Pokey wanted none of it. Before, he had whimpered a bit when he'd been pinched or restrained. Now he became vociferous.

Climbing up on the roof wire of his cage, he shouted his protest. First he tried a hoo-hoo-hoo, sounding like a barking dog. Then a petulant squeal. Then a mournful wail, like a hungry baby. Finally, he subsided into a hurt little sniffle, as if to let us know that the cage was giving him pneumonia.

He complained all night but we didn't give in. He's been in the cage ever since, although the moral victory is his. Somebody usually takes him out every few hours. He's just too much fun to let alone.

I used to let him ride my typewriter carriage, for instance, until he became too big. He still shuffles into my study when he hears it going and climbs up on my lap hopefully. I put him back down on the floor but he shinnies right back. Then I have to call for someone to rescue me.

Pokey loves to play tag, too, as long as he can be "it." He runs after us as fast as his short legs can carry him. As soon as he catches one of us, someone else will stamp his feet and Pokey will gallop after him.

A local forester heard about our strange pet and came to see for himself. "Porcupines," he told me as he watched Pokey chase the children on the lawn, "never play tag. They are completely antisocial, stupid, destructive, and uninteresting. That's what we were told in forestry school. Obviously, your porcupine has never been to school."

No matter where he is, Pokey responds at once to his name. We often put him in a tree to exercise his claws and keep his rodent teeth worn down. When we want him again, we merely speak to him. Sampling the air with nose and ears, he decides exactly where we are, even if his myopic eyes cannot pick us out. Then he faithfully hunches backwards down the limb, his teeth chattering in anticipation, feeling along with his sensitive muscular tail. Once in our arms, he gently nibbles at a wrist or finger, as if to tell us how glad he is to be back again.

His feet are marvelous tools. Armed with four long, crescent-shaped claws in front, five in the rear, they are flat and black, like little thumbless monkey hands. They can get a surprising grip on a branch. And so strongly hooked are the claws that he can walk along while hanging upside down under a branch, like a sloth.

Pokey walks flat-footed, like a little bear. When he's really going somewhere, he carries his tail tilted almost straight up. Often he walks a few steps on his hind legs, using the tail as the third point of a tripod. With his heavy gray coat of fur and quills extending right to his hands and feet, he reminds Peg of a foot-high little man in a snowsuit.

Can Pokey throw his quills? Actually, he cannot. But in effect he can. Once, in his war dance, he slapped his tail against a chair leg. A few quills snapped loose and flew across the room. But ordinarily you'd have to touch a porky to get even a single quill. The spines of full-grown adults—six inches or longer—stay with their owner until some foolhardy creature rams against their tiny barbed points and leaps back with a few dozen.

The porcupine merely grows new quills to replace those he loses. Meantime, the backward-pointing barbs cause the quills to work steadily deeper into his attacker. Once they have caught hold, they move in one direction only—inward.

Actually, we don't even worry about his quills. We always pick Pokey up by putting our hands beneath him. His belly is as soft as a spaniel's ear, for its hairs have not differentiated into the slender white shafts which cover the rest of his body from nose to tail. It's the belly that is sought out by the fisher, large cousin of the weasel, and the porcupine's only effective natural enemy.

People ask me how I think such a prickly baby can be born without hurting the mother. Probably the answer lies in the softening effect of water on the baby quills. Soaked in its own natal fluid, the single newborn porcupine must be no more spiny than a pound of wet sawdust. And, like a puppy, it's encased in a membrane when born, offering the mother further protection.

How porcupines mate I do not know. Nor have I been able to find the answer in any of my books. But, knowing how Pokey can keep his spears flat against his body when necessary, I'd say that mating would pose no great problem. We have quite a number of wild porcupines here in the Green Mountains of Vermont. Perhaps next autumn I'll find a wild one, release Pokey near it, and make a note of what happens.

Scores of people—many of them total strangers—have stopped at our farmhouse to see our unusual pet. Half a year old, he weighs about five pounds. So he is about half-grown. He's so durable, according to my books, that we can expect him to live about ten years.

Nature's Rascals

You'll probably never see an animal laugh. Apparently man is the only living thing that can burst into a loud guffaw. But that doesn't mean that some other creatures don't get just as much kick out of life—often at the expense of others.

Take the raccoon, for instance. There's one less than fifty feet away from me at this moment. She was given to us by a Vermont neighbor who found her, an orphan baby, chased into a tree by dogs. We've had her nearly a year now and she's near the top of our rascal list. "As curious as a coon" is an old expression and Scamper lives up to her reputation.

One day she got into our attic and took all the old clothes out of the trunks. Then she stuck her little handlike forepaw up through a tiny hole in the roof, enlarging it so much that the next rain sent us scurrying for buckets. Another time, Scamper found a box of eggs among groceries in our car and methodically opened the eggs, drained the contents, and puddled the eggs with her front paws. In the wild, a raccoon which comes across the nest of a grouse or pheasant will do exactly the same thing.

And any camper can tell you what happens when a raccoon gets into a woodland cabin. It will pull pots off the shelves, open every package in sight, and unwind kitchen toweling the length of the floor.

Then there's the raccoon's huge cousin. Nearsighted, lumbering, yet amazingly swift and catlike when it wants to be, the two-hundred-pound black bear takes over where his fifteen-pound relative stops. If he comes to a hollow tree and hears the humming sound of bees inside it, he'll spend half a day tearing it apart to get at the honey. A few stings on the nose are about the worst he may expect, for his thick fur is good protection. And if the tree happens to be a telephone pole with the bees merely the humming of the wires, the pole may get clawed in two before bruin gives up. A bear may spend ten minutes beating the life out of an inoffensive little bush that strikes his fancy. Or, if he happens to find a nest of hornets, he'll rip the earth open to get at the hornets' grubs. Then he walks away, leaving things in a fine state for the next unsuspecting passerby.

Sharing the woods with the bear is another creature for whom even bruin steps aside. The porcupine's weakness is that he's a gourmet. He likes to sample assorted items, especially if they have a dash of salt or sugar, for example, ax handles which have been touched by sweaty hands or, here in Vermont, the equipment used in making the famous maple syrup. A few miles from my house hundreds of dollars' worth of ski-tow rope out in the woods has been nibbled to a frazzle by porkies.

A few years ago, we had a porcupine—a prickly little baby —that had been orphaned in a forest fire. "Pokey" became as tame as a kitten and never stuck us with those barbed quills. He was perfectly housebroken, so we gave him the run of the place—until he discovered what those four yellow chisel teeth were for. One night we heard a crunching downstairs in the dining room. We raced down and snapped on the lights. There was Pokey, blinking pleasantly while his eyes got used to the glare. And two of the arms of our fancy dining-room chairs had taken on a hand-carved look.

Aesop's Fables tell of the wily fox and his tricks. Almost any outdoors man can go Aesop one better from his own experience. I know of a fox that got a dog to chase it out onto the thin ice of a pond. Then, while the lightweight fox scampered to safety, the heavier dog broke through and spent the next five minutes floundering to shore in the icy water while the fox watched from the opposite bank. A man who raises sheep tells how a fox will sometimes spring onto the back of one sheep, then jump from one animal to another, spreading panic through the whole flock although it doesn't harm the sheep at all.

Practical jokers aren't limited to the furry set, of course. You can't judge a bird by its plumage. One of the best-dressed birds in North America is also one of the woodland's biggest headaches. Splendid in its coat of clearest blue and spotless white, the blue jay looks as innocent as a six-year-old on the first day of school. But turn your back and things begin to happen.

Blue jays peck at the tails of sleeping cats. They steal the food out of a dog's dish. They come to our bird feeder in winter—sometimes more than a dozen of them—and stuff themselves with food while the smaller birds have to wait for what's left. And they can make a sound so much like a hawk that small birds fly for cover. Last summer we were happy when a pair of yellow warblers built a nest in the bushes near our house. One day after the eggs had hatched, the warblers were flying in and out of the bush in great excitement with chirps of alarm. When we ran to the bush, there stood a blue jay, calmly picking the warbler babies out and dropping them to the ground. (Luckily, the earth below was soft so the babies had landed unharmed.)

All the jays and their relatives seem to be feathered delinquents. One camper at Crater Lake National Park had a longer vacation than he'd intended. It took him most of the morning to rescue his car keys from the top of a tree where a Clark's nutcracker had left them.

Magpies delight in stealing bright objects, too. Their nests have contained tin cups, silverware, compacts, even a pair of thick eyeglasses. Sometimes the magpie sits outside the hole of a prairie dog and chases the peaceful burrowing rodent inside every time the little animal sticks his nose out.

Although the crow takes fine care of its own family, it seems to regard almost every other living creature as made for sport. We had a little puppy which we tied to a tree in the backyard. The puppy yelped and cried as if being outside on that June day was going to give him influenza. Suddenly, the puppy's wailing doubled in volume. We ran outside, thinking he was tangled in his leash. But only part of the noise was coming from our pup. There in the tree sat two crows, looking down at him. Every time he yelped, they answered him right back in perfect imitation!

If crows find a sleeping owl, they carry on with such a cawing and flapping that the owl is forced to fly away. Even then, the crows fly ahead, behind, alongside, diving and rushing until the owl is literally mobbed in his attempt to escape.

Don't ask a farmer what he thinks of crows. A crow will sit right on the head of a scarecrow and watch the farmer plant his cornfield again—and then will pull up the corn a second time.

One of the greatest rascals of all time has been around since long before the days of the dinosaur. The astounding cockroach is bold enough to make its way into almost every kind of dwelling known to man—from airplanes and skyscrapers to submarines. Flat and tough-shelled, the roach can slip into almost any crack and can survive on crumbs in an old bread wrapper or on a few drops left in a soda bottle. It's not quite the same as feasting on broken dinosaur eggs and fillet of mammoth, but the cockroach doesn't seem to mind the change!

Once I had to spend several weeks in the tropics. As soon as the sun went down, two long feelers would emerge from a knothole in a wall near my bed. If I went to poke at the cockroach with a stick, those delicate feelers would somehow sense it and disappear before I could touch them.

One night I turned out the light but remained quietly seated on the bed. After a few minutes, I snapped the light on and caught sight of him nibbling his way into a candy wrapper. In reaching for the wrapper, I flipped him upside down and discovered one more reason why cockroaches have been able to survive for so long. Instead of waving his legs helplessly in the air as a beetle might have done, the roach stretched them out flat. This enabled his toes to just touch the wooden floor. "Running" wildly upside down, he escaped into a space between two boards while I watched in astonishment.

There are rascals among the lower creatures, too. Sunfish will surround the gravelly nest of the black bass, waiting for a chance to dash in and seize an egg when the parent is not on guard. Sunfish also have a way of nibbling at a worm without getting hooked.

If you live along the seacoast, you've probably seen plenty of crabs. Some seem to have a double measure of mischief in their makeup. They pinch the fins of fish that swim too close and pull baby oysters off rocks.

One summer day on the Maine coast, I watched a crab make things lively for a group of black-shelled mussels in about a foot of water. Their shells were partly open to take in tiny floating bits of food. The crab crept slowly over their shells. When it found a mussel that was partly open, it quickly poked at its tender flesh with a claw. Then, before the mussel could snap shut, it pulled the claw out and went on to the next. It did this over and over, almost as if it enjoyed keeping as many shells closed as it could. The crab's probing was probably partly a search for a little food. Sometimes, however, it gets *too* curious and gets its claw caught as it reaches down inside the shell of a mussel or clam. Then it must break the claw off and slowly grow a new one.

The spirit of discovery is strong in many wild creatures. Yet many of their antics, for lack of a better explanation, seem to fit best under the heading of "mischief for the sake of mischief." So, even though man is about the only living being that can smile or burst into laughter, sometimes you get the feeling that nature's rascals may get the last laugh after all.

Uncanny Cat

THE WATER was creeping above my ankles, but I didn't dare look down. Even though uncornered wildcats aren't supposed to attack people, this one could be different. Surprised by a boy only ten feet away, he might well figure he was cornered.

I'd been stepping from one hummock to another in a swamp, looking for turtles and frogs. As I put my weight on each hummock, it would sink. So my progress had been marked by a strange ballet as I jockeyed my way toward a little grassy island twice the size of a kitchen table. I was just two leaps away when I raised my head for a last check of its position. It was then that I was stopped by those blazing eyes.

His mouth opened in a soundless snarl. Those four white fangs looked long and terribly sharp. Brown-and-white streaks gave his face a look of savagery as he laid his ears back against his head. The yellow eyes narrowed until the pupils were just slits. And there we both stood.

Then came the uncanny part. While my heart pounded and his face etched itself on my mind, I suddenly discovered he was gone. He hadn't bounded away or plunged into the water. He had just faded from sight. Those eyes had melted into the background while they held me spellbound. The open mouth somehow became a dry leaf. Those facial streaks turned into the brown grass of the April swamp.

Only the gentle swaying of the vegetation told me I hadn't dreamed the whole affair.

Whether he finally swam away or still lurked, hidden, I do not know. Nor did I try to find out. That was my first meeting with a wildcat. It lasted only about ten seconds. But they were a long, indelible ten seconds. Since then I've talked with other people who have met wildcats, and nearly every one of them reports the same reaction—a steady, unblinking stare and an unhurried, ghostlike retreat. They all use the same word to describe the encounter: unforgettable!

What are the chances of the average person seeing a wildcat? Perhaps this question should be turned around: What are the odds that a camouflaged wildcat might peek out from its swamp or thicket at *you*?

The answer may be a bit surprising. In the southwestern scrub, you may come under the gaze of a wildcat as often as once a week during a camping jaunt. A rancher friend of mine hunts wildcats and gets about one a week, while in my own Vermont woodlands, one very successful hunter bagged an even dozen in twice that many weeks.

Apparently, if one is looking at you—whether you're aware of it or not—it's only curiosity. A neighbor of mine had the unnerving experience of being followed by a wildcat for more than a mile as he walked through the New Hampshire woods with his little dog. The dog bristled and growled and clung so closely that his master finally picked him up and carried him. Occasionally they saw the wildcat peacefully trotting along behind them, apparently having no harmful intentions whatsoever.

Barring such an episode, the opportunity of glimpsing a wildcat in the eastern woodlands may occur perhaps once in ten or fifteen years. In the more open South and West, says my rancher friend, the average person out in the bush may see a wildcat once a year.

The creature has such a grip on the popular imagination, however, that you're probably not far from other "wildcats" even as you read this. You may have a Wildcat parked in your garage or resting on your boat trailer. Marine and Navy pilots flew Wildcats at the enemy in World War II. There are Wildcat chain saws, Wildcat motorcycles, and—intriguing as the prospect sounds—a Wildcat Sewer Service in a town not far from my home.

If you've driven through the Catskill Mountains, you've been in wildcat country, too, in more ways than one. Henry Hudson dubbed the area's rushing river *Kaats Kill*—Dutch for "Wildcat Creek." My wife Peg and I once stayed at the Wildcat Motel in one of the region's little towns. It was a singularly uneventful visit.

There are wildcat (take-a-chance) oil wells, wildcat stocks, wildcat enterprises of many kinds. Every one of our wars since the Revolution has engaged the services of Wildcat regiments, squadrons, or other fighting units. And doubtless nearly every state has its fighting Wildcat high-school and college athletic teams, even in areas which may not be blessed by the presence of the real animal.

At first glance, a wildcat looks ordinary enough. It's about half again as large as a good-sized tomcat. But as you look closer, you realize that's where the resemblance stops. Averaging perhaps twenty pounds, the wildcat seems to be a miniature cross between a tiger and a leopard, with a bit of mountain lion thrown in. Its rust-brown coat shows spots and flecks above and a suggestion of dark stripes below, blending into a white belly. Heavy lines on its wide-flaring cheek fur break up the outline of its face so it can see without being seen. A little tuft of hair on each ear serves as an antenna which is sensitive to sounds or air currents. Its whiskers, bedded in delicate nerves, may lie back—or reach out to determine if a certain opening will admit its body.

There's nothing quite like a wildcat in action. While it's ordinarily so peace-loving that even a Chihuahua could probably put it to flight, once aroused it can whip nearly any dog alive. A flick of powerful muscles, and those velvet paws suddenly bristle with eighteen knives—four claws on each hind foot and five in front. Spitting defiance, it offers the enemy one last chance to retreat. The ears and sensitive whiskers are laid so flat against the head that they seem to disappear. Then it springs to the attack, clinging with front claws, roweling and digging with the rear ones, biting deep with its fangs.

Indeed, a wildcat sometimes hates to quit. Cornered by more than one enemy, it leaps from one to the other in such a blaze of claws and teeth and fur that its bewildered tormentors may soon become the tormented. After seeing one wildcat in action, I know now what the pioneers meant when they said something was "as easy as letting go of a wildcat."

But there's the lighter side. As with other cats, its tail twitches when the owner is excited. Somehow, though, the wildcat's little six-inch appendage merely looks ridiculous as it flips back and forth. It's this afterthought of nature which has earned it a second name—bobcat.

It is also called bobcat for another reason. A running wildcat bobs up and down like a rabbit. Its relatively long hind legs give it a gait better suited to a short dash than a long run. Hunters know this and count on a bobcat to take refuge in a tree after their hounds are fast on the trail. Otherwise it might go hard for the dogs, indeed.

The Canada lynx of the North is the only other American cat resembling the bobcat. Its average size is slightly larger (up to thirty-five pounds), though some bobcats are fully as large. Stub-tailed like its southern relative, the lynx has longer ear tufts and a more uniform brownish coat. Its great padded feet grow "snowshoes" of stiff fur in winter. Of course, the bobcat would scarcely need snowshoes at the southern limit of its range, in central Mexico—nor, for that matter, over most of its territory. This covers much of the continental United States, the bobcat ranging north to overlap the lynx near the Canadian border.

Scientists, in distinguishing between the two, named the

bobcat *Lynx rufus*—which, naturally, means "the rufus-colored lynx," although individuals in southwestern chaparrals and canyons may be nearly as pale as desert sand. When biologists came to the Canadian lynx, however, they neatly side-stepped a description of the gray-brown animal by calling it *Lynx canadensis*. Otherwise the two animals are much the same, although the Canada lynx is more retiring and less able to abide the presence of man.

The modern bobcat is the result of a long period of adjustment in nature. Over the eons the cat family evolved from some remote Old World ancestor: tigers and lions to catch zebra and antelope, mountain lions to catch deer, the Canada lynx to prey on the snowshoe hare, little Asiatic and African cats to catch birds and mice and give rise to our household felines. Somewhere, perhaps eight million years ago, the forerunners of the bobcat began to develop a taste for the forerunners of our rats and rabbits. They've been together ever since.

Even though today's bobcat can take the presence of man in small doses—setting up residence in overgrown brushland or making nightly rounds along gravel roads—you'll be lucky to see even one living specimen in the wild. Its eyes and ears are easily keen enough to warn of your coming, although its nose is less sensitive. And what I learned as a boy apparently still holds: No wildcat in its right mind would, unprovoked, attack a human being.

Once in a while, however, one makes a mistake. Stanley P. Young, who has known these animals for years, tells in his fascinating book *The Bobcat of North America* of a hunter who went out after coyotes in Texas. Settling down beside a bush, the hunter waited for some potential target to show itself. To stack the odds in his favor, he decided to call a few times in an imitation of a coyote.

He got more results than he planned for. With a yowl, something hit him in the back. It was a full-grown bobcat.

Claws out, teeth bared, she lit into him until she discovered her error. Then she bounded away.

Shaken, the hunter tried to piece together what had happened. After a search he found a den of bobcat kittens nearby. She had been protecting her family from this invading enemy—something she would not have done if she'd realized the "coyote" was a human. She'd merely have slunk away and he wouldn't have been the wiser.

Though bobcats are hard to see, they're nowhere near as hard to hear. They use the same language as a domestic tabby on a back fence only several times more vocal. They howl, snarl, spit, and scream like a demented woman. One night my wife and I were on the edge of a Vermont lake, gazing at the glow of a little fire on the opposite shore, when a bobcat let go in the woods behind us. No sooner had the yowls stopped echoing than we could see figures frantically running around the fire. In a few minutes the "protective" flames were blazing high enough to light up half the lake.

In late winter almost any reasonably wild area may be blessed by a bobcat. This is when the two sexes start seeking companionship. The male, normally content with a bachelor's lot, may expand his normal ten-square-mile cruising range to as much as one hundred fifty square miles during the mating season. His future mate starts on her own circle.

Occasionally each stops to deposit a few drops of urine at a convenient spot in the trail. This is, apparently, the bobcat's way of saying "I was here and I'm available." When another cat comes along, it investigates the urine spot. Then it solemnly deposits a message of its own: "Me, too."

When the two sexes get together eventually, the results are apt to be deafening. Yowling and squalling, the bobcats scream sweet nothings at each other. When the tender moment passes, however, they lapse into a stealthy silence. This of course bodes ill for rabbits—a favorite food—as well as for mice, snakes, and ground-nesting birds.

For nearly two months they hunt together. Although they can climb well, most of their hunting is done on the ground. Often they'll try several techniques before the final one is chosen. Coming across a family of wild turkeys or roving quail, the bobcats will study the birds' line of march. Then they run silently ahead to ambush their prey at a favorable spot. Wildcats will attack deer as well—usually starvation-weakened animals during late winter—and have been known to bring down a mature buck ten times their size. The cat clings like a demon at the neck, biting for the jugular vein while the frantic prey runs and tries to dislodge its assailant against a tree or rock.

Finally the day comes for the mother wildcat's confinement. She announces the happy event to her mate in typical wildcat fashion—with a spitfire attack that sends him packing. Then, finding a suitable hollow beneath an overturned stump or under a ledge, she goes about gathering a few wisps of grass or leaves to serve as a nest.

Her mate philosophically goes back to the bachelor life he left two months earlier, unless, as a lady biologist told me with an obvious sense of the unfairness of it all, "he happens to come across another unmated female. Then he may take up with her for a while."

The kits are born fully furred and scarcely larger than domestic kittens.

A forester once showed me a wildcat den in upstate New York. It was beneath an old log on a wooded hillside. The three kits were cute, each about the size of my fist. They looked about a week old, mottled brown and buff, with bleary blue eyes just beginning to open. It was easy to see what fun they would be in a couple of weeks, hard to believe what terrors they'd be by the end of the summer.

When the kits are a few weeks old, the cat family's well-known curiosity asserts itself. They begin to waddle after their mother as she heads for the door of the den.

A friend of mine once watched the departure of a nursing

female from beneath a ledge on a hillside. "It was a nice June evening," he recalled, "and I'd been sitting on a slope, listening to the birds. Suddenly I saw a movement on the opposite hill and put my binoculars on the spot. It was an old lady wildcat just leaving her den.

"Right behind her," he continued, "I could see the faces of three kittens. She stopped and stared at them and they disappeared. But when she started to walk away they showed up again. So she walked back, took a swipe at the nearest one, and tumbled them all back into the hole like bowling pins. I guess they got the message that time. I watched for half an hour and never saw them again."

But they were probably back at the same stunt the next day. Wildcat babies are as irrepressible as most other kittens. As they learn to use their muscles and needle-sharp claws, they stalk each other until, with a bound, they tumble in a heap. If the mother is basking at the entrance to the den they may all sneak up on her. Each kitten's stubby tail twitches at its own speed. Then they pounce on their "victim" with savage little growls.

At this stage they're occasionally discovered and taken home by a hiker or camper. "I've known them to make wonderful pets while they were young," a forester told me, "and a rare one might stay tame right through adult age. When I went to college in Idaho, one of the professors had a bobcat that lived in his house. It had wonderful manners—even perched on the edge of the toilet bowl at the proper time.

"One man I know takes his bobcat around and lectures about it," he continued. "But bobcats have also been known to turn on their masters without warning. It's just like anything you find in the wild—it's a wild animal, and don't you forget it."

Sometime in mid-summer the kits change their milk diet for one of meat. Now the mother allows the father back into her good graces for a while. Both parents may bring a rabbit or squirrel to the den—the prey only slightly injured so the kits can learn to catch it. Or they may take the family on short excursions, during which the kits stalk beetles and wind-tossed leaves with comical seriousness.

All summer the mother teaches her family the many arts of hunting. Like most members of the cat family, bobcats rely more on their eyes and ears than their noses. They learn to unthread the maze of rabbit trails in a woodland until they come to the "form" or cubbyhole where a rabbit may be crouching. A few bewildering misses show them that they cannot dash into the middle of a flock of grouse but must concentrate on a single bird. Pouncing on tufts of grass with all four feet, they carefully lift each paw to see if they have surprised a mouse. But contrary to popular belief, they seldom lie in wait in a tree for luckless animals which happen to pass beneath.

Like most cats, they have to investigate everything. Although they're largely night prowlers as adults, bobcat kittens explore the daytime world, too. They may sit in a ring and solemnly study the activity of an anthill, then just as solemnly deposit a bit of excreta on it as a fillip of their own. They may carefully turn over a pebble, roll it along a path like a domestic tabby with a ball of yarn, or dip an inquiring paw into a rain puddle. Sometimes they'll wade right into a swamp, batting away at whirligig beetles. They will take to water with less distaste than their civilized cousins do. And at any moment all this may turn into frolic if they run across a few sprigs of catnip. The minty weed has the same effect on the bobcats as on housecats—they roll and purr and go slightly balmy.

With the onset of winter, each wildcat youngster strikes out for itself. The parting ceremony may be just a simple case of the kittens wandering off or it may be precipitated by a whopping family squabble. At any rate the three-quarters-grown kit, though still a year away from the adult size of thirty inches and twenty-plus pounds for males (with females a bit smaller), is nearly mature and able to take care of himself. If he lasts through the winter, he may add his own serenade to that of his parents and littermates the following spring. But, although the bobcat has few natural enemies, survival is not a foregone conclusion. If he cannot find a reasonably wild area of deserted farmland or back-country brushland to call his own, he will keep moving.

This exposes him to a number of hazards. He is quite literally caught off base. Bobcats often cover a kill and return to it. But a bobcat without his own territory must live a hand-to-mouth existence. Members of his own kind want no squatters and tell him to move elsewhere. Thus he faces the threat that lurks for almost every creature in the wild—a shortage of elbow room.

Eventually the wandering bobcat may come to the outskirts of a farm with a chicken house or with a few lambs in a pasture. Such a bonanza, of course, soon brings him afoul of man himself. Then he finds a price on his head. Bobcat bounties, in fact, date back to the 1700s.

To collect a bounty it was once necessary to surrender a portion of the body—often the ears—to a village clerk or other authority. But a clever trapper could cut three or four pairs of "ears" out of the belly of a bobcat. Then he'd let them ripen in the sun. When he took them to the town hall they'd be so rich that the poor clerk would hold them at arm's length—if he could get near them at all—and end up paying several bounties for one bobcat.

When word of such unlawful ways got around, it became necessary for the bounty hunter to display a bobcat nose. However, a little backwoods plastic surgery on the paws resulted in bobcats with four extra "noses"—one for each foot. Payment for bobcat tails turned out to be precisely that, with the de-tailed adult allowed to run free and raise a litter of tailed youngsters.

It finally became necessary to surrender the whole animal to collect a bounty. This was fine for everybody but the poor official who found himself with a bunch of carcasses for disposal. And sometimes the easiest way to dispose of them was to take them to another official—and thereby collect a second bounty.

Such mixups, however, are nothing compared to the state of affairs the bobcat finds itself in today. Feeling runs so high that laws may change overnight, but at this writing the bobcat finds itself virtually cursed on Tuesdays and Thursdays and blessed on Mondays, Wednesdays, and Fridays.

A few examples: About fifteen states still pay bounties on bobcats, either throughout the state or in individual towns and counties. Some Connecticut towns, for instance, still offer a bobcat bounty even though they've actually had nothing more menacing than a skunk at a garbage pail since the last century. My own adopted state of Vermont dutifully pays a reward for every departed bobcat. Apparently in defiance of inflation, which many a Vermonter lays to every administration since Coolidge, the bounty has been resolutely lowered from $20 in the post-Coolidge era to $10 today.

On the other side, several Canadian provinces recognize the wildcat as a furbearer, its hide worth up to $20 for coats, gloves, stoles, and even items like the little three-pelt rug which I purchased at an auction.

Nor is that all. "In most places, rabbits and wildcats just naturally go together," a game warden told me. "But sportsmen, finding evidence of an occasional bobcat attack on grouse or quail, have tended to overlook that fact. In one place in the Southwest they bountied the wildcat so intensively that they finally had to turn around and slap a closed season on it to keep a check on the jackrabbit population."

How has all the furore affected the number of bobcats? "Despite the bounty," says Jack H. Berryman, chief of the Division of Wildlife Services of the Federal Bureau of Sport Fisheries and Wildlife, "bobcat numbers in general appear to be constant and may even be increasing over much of their range."

Exactly what those numbers are is anybody's guess. The

ten thousand or so which part with their mottled coats—and their lives—in the United States each year may represent one-fifth of the actual population, according to one estimate. Another guess says this is merely one-tenth of the total number.

It all adds up to one fact: Unless caught in a trap or treed by dogs, the wraithlike wildcat just doesn't stand around waiting to be counted.

Even its tracks are confusing. Rounded, two inches in diameter, and placed in single file, they are spaced about nine inches apart and could almost be those of an outsized fox— until you suddenly realize that there aren't any claw marks to a bobcat track. Besides, nothing but a bobcat could lay down the trail I followed through a cedar swamp last winter —along a snow-covered log, up the slanting stub of a six-foot branch perhaps three inches in diameter at the tip, then out through space in a five-foot leap, the cat landing precisely on the tip of a similar stub without once clutching to maintain its balance. Then it walked nonchalantly back down to earth and off through the bushes.

Unaware of all the confusion he's caused ever since he first stared down at the forerunners of Ethan Allen, Davy Crockett, and Daniel Boone, the bobcat goes his ornery, independent way. He lends his name and his reputation to athletic teams all over the country. He sends delicious chills along the spines of campers who fancy they can see his eyes shining beyond the fire.

Those same eyes, with pupils which can expand enormously to see in the dark or contract to pinpoints in the sunshine, are so keen that Indians thought the bobcat could see through rocks, trees, even hillsides. The fastidious way it often covers its excreta gave rise to an Indian belief that its urine turns to precious jewels. And so the bobcat travels surrounded by legend.

Actually, chances are slim that you'll ever see a bobcat. But then you could be as lucky as two friends of mine who

73

once saw a wildcat up a telephone pole in broad daylight on a country road. Or you could equal my experience and stumble across one that glares at you with a soundless snarl from a tussock of swamp grass, only to evaporate like a mist while you swear he's still standing there.

Which is doubtless why the French trappers gave him the name he still bears in parts of Canada today: *chat mystérieux*—that uncanny cat.

Don't Mention My Name
to a Skunk

WE WERE sitting on the back porch of Don's home in the country. Cement mixers, old planks, sawhorses decorated the yard. "Tomorrow," Don began, "we'll start on the garage—"

But he never finished. Instead, he pointed soundlessly toward the corner of the house. A skunk had ambled out of the bushes in the waning light. Absorbed in its wanderings, it had made its way to where a few boards were spread out on the ground.

As we watched, the skunk walked out on one of the boards. Then, accompanied by a groan of despair from my friend, it began to sink into the ground. At the same time the other end of the board rose majestically into the air. We got one glimpse of a wildly waving tail and then the board dropped back in place. But no skunk.

I was impressed. "Where'd he go?"

Another groan from Don. "Into the well."

The workmen had been digging a pit in the yard. The old farm's never-failing spring had failed and the pit was a fresh attempt at water. They'd covered it with boards when they'd finished digging in the hope that it would fill in a few days. And one of the loose boards had dumped the skunk.

Warily we circled the hole with its unseen occupant. There was a little breeze blowing but we caught no whiff of skunk. At least the ultimate catastrophe hadn't befallen.

Now the question was how to prevent it from befalling. Our little black-and-white friend, we figured, must be (1) stunned from his seven-foot fall, (2) swimming in Don's drinking water, or (3) a little of both.

At any rate, he had to be rescued. After changing into some old clothes, I grabbed a wire basket and a rope. Then I advanced to the battle.

While Don held a flashlight, I gingerly pulled the boards away from the opening. And there was our adversary, neither stunned nor swimming. There wasn't any water to swim in and his little jaunt hadn't bothered him at all. He just blinked at us for a moment—and went back to dining on a luckless frog that had made it into the hole sometime before he did.

Don's dry well was obviously better at collecting wildlife than water. For lack of any better plan of action, we put a few chunks of hamburger in the wire basket. We lowered it down on two ropes and let it come to rest on its side in the well. Then we gently prodded the little creature with a stick.

As if it had all been rehearsed, the skunk obligingly walked into the basket. Then we took up slack on the rope until we had him hanging in his open cage like a pendulum. He shifted uneasily when he felt it sway but soon went back to his hamburger.

Praying the food would last long enough, we gently eased him up to the top in his make-shift elevator. We swung him away from the hole and set him down. He finished his meal, looked at us for a moment, and then shuffled away.

Incredible? Not at all. It was completely in character for the two-toned little fellow. For, in spite of his reputation, the skunk is one of nature's most ardent pacifists.

Like many another pacifist, he hoists a distinctive banner —that huge, feathery tail. But he supports his position with a weapon so terrible that even wolves and wildcats back away from him respectfully like slaves before an emperor.

Since that day at Don's well—which finally did fill with pure, nonskunky water, by the way—I've had two other occasions to rescue skunks at close hand. Both of them turned out equally well.

The first occasion was when a skunk was caught by its foot in a steel trap. It waited alertly, tail raised, while I reached down with my hands and released it. Another skunk was more of a problem. Poking around the trash barrels of the village where I live, it had caught its head in a tin can. The neighbors called me when they heard it banging around in the street at dawn. I took the call in stride; as a naturalist I get these calls day and night.

I spoke words of assurance until I gained enough of the skunk's attention so that it stopped thrashing and listened to my voice. I touched it first from a safe distance with a fishing pole to test its reactions and finally got the courage to kneel beside it. Stroking its back, I was amazed to find how small and vibrant the little body was beneath that thick, glossy fur. It felt like a warm, slender cat.

Gingerly I grasped the tin can. It seemed fairly loose. Still speaking words of comfort and consolation, I positioned one hand just in front of those sturdy little shoulders. I put the other hand on the tin can. Then, holding my breath and turning my head away, I pulled.

The skunk came free, all right. I'd put such desperation into the effort that the can flew clattering up the street and the skunk went tumbling down. Righting himself, he surveyed me soberly for a minute. Then, after rubbing his head with his paw, he hurried off to bed. Skunks are nocturnal creatures and apparently he had had quite a night.

Although all my contacts with skunks have been, shall we say, uneventful, those two marble-sized glands buried beneath the base of the tail can pack even more wallop than many people realize. All that horrendous smell comes from three or four drops of liquid, seldom more. It may be shot out

77

as either a jet or a fine mist. If it hits the eyes, it may blind them, sometimes even permanently. And a skunk can spray several times in succession.

Often the skunk flips itself around in a tight letter "U" so that both its head and tail are facing the enemy. But it can fire from any position—even, as one game warden sadly assured me, when it's being held by the tail. Apparently a skunk hoisted aloft by that gorgeous plumed black-and-white appendage usually withholds its artillery for a very sensible reason—it doesn't want to get all smelled up either.

And this brings up a point: A skunk apparently dislikes its aroma nearly as much as other animals do. This probably helps explain the occasions when one of the little wood pussies should have fired but didn't. Things might have been at too close quarters, even for a skunk, whose weapon is accurate only up to about ten feet.

It may help explain, too, why a friend of mine has had a skunk for more than eighteen months now in his Manhattan apartment—and his neighbors are none the wiser.

"We found her one May day in the Adirondacks," he told me. "We heard this chattering noise at the roots of an old stump. Sounded like a sparrow. Apparently her mother had been killed and she was the only baby left alive. She was naked and blind—about the size of a newborn kitten. We wouldn't have known what she was except for a faint little 'V' ingrained right in her skin and running back on either side to her tail. Then, too, there was the way she tried to fire at us when she heard us coming—even though her squirt gun was still loaded only with blanks."

They took her home and raised her on sweetened milk fed with a medicine dropper. In answer to my question as to whether she'd been denatured by a veterinarian, he looked shocked.

"Of course not. You know how peaceful skunks are, anyway. And why take away her only means of protection?

Then if she ever got lost, even a sleepy alley cat could kill her."

He did have one close call, though. Animals aren't allowed in his apartment building. So he has to smuggle Lilac out under his overcoat at odd hours to enjoy a few stolen moments on the tiny lawn near the street. Early one Sunday morning after such a jaunt, he got back on the self-service elevator with the skunk safely hidden in his chest.

"Just as I was about to close the elevator door," he recalls, "a portly lady got on the elevator, too. I lost my balance when the car started and fell against her. And do you know what she did? She barked."

"Barked?"

"Yep. Or at least you'd have thought so. Then she kind of looked at me with a funny grin and patted her tummy. 'Billy,' she said, and a dog's head came poking out of her coat. She was keeping a pet on the sly, too."

My friend grinned. "But that wasn't the worst of it. When Billy barked, I could feel Lilac stiffen. 'Oh, oh,' I said to myself, 'here we go.'"

But Lilac remained a little lady throughout the ascent. So, as my friend, who obviously must remain anonymous, says, the neighbors haven't yet gotten wind of his unusual pet.

Still more daring is the case of another friend, the late Stuart Huckins of Duxbury, Massachusetts. Daring, that is, unless you know your skunks. For Stuart and his wife Olga have served supper to as many as six fully armed wild skunks at once—right in their living room.

It started with an event familiar to many a suburban dweller—a skunk at the garbage can. As they were both animal lovers, the Huckinses put out a bit of food for their visitor. Soon they had two skunks. Then they put the food in a pan on the back steps.

The skunks were so well-behaved that the Huckinses took courage. They fixed the back entrance with a free-swinging

79

screen door and scattered food right across the threshold.

From the first, the skunks showed that they were individualists. They preferred to feed in separate parts of the room and, later, in several rooms. Hence, before they had developed distinct personalities they were christened "the desk skunk," "the kitchen skunk," "the sitting-room skunk," and so on. Later they were endowed with names like "Blacky" and "Whitey" and "Little Black Spot."

Soon Blacky and Whitey and their friends were regular members of the family. Then one night Whitey showed up with four tiny replicas of herself—two-toned coats, feathery tails, and all.

That was three years ago. Since then Whitey has become a grandmother. Sometimes all three generations have come for the nightly handout.

The first time I visited them, I got there well before dusk. Then, as twilight approached, there was a scratching at the back door. In a moment there were three skunks right in the living room. Olga put a pan of dog food and cereal on the rug. The skunks daintily nibbled at it, cleaning up every crumb. They even took cookies from my hand.

When I asked the inevitable question, Stuart grinned. "Never had a mistake in the house yet," he said. "And we even had a free-loading raccoon last year who tried to horn in, too. The skunks'd stamp their front feet and raise their tails at him. But they always managed to stop short of the point of no return."

Somehow the raccoon and the skunks worked up a truce and the Huckins' home remains unscathed. In fact, it has even benefited. After the skunks have finished their evening meal, they go puttering off over the lawn, investigating every tussock and clump of dirt for a grub or a beetle—for skunks are tireless insect hunters.

And "puttering" is nearly the only word you can use for a skunk's progress. Peering nearsightedly with little black beady eyes at its surroundings, a skunk must live forever in a world with a horizon only a few feet away. Everything beyond that is blurred. So most of the time it pokes along, nose to the ground, plumed tail lightly dragging, often mumbling to itself in a contented singsong as it searches for food.

A keen nose and strong claws help the five-pounder in his quest. And, since he's not at all fussy, food is usually easy to find—from ground-dwelling grubs to ground-nesting birds. In fact, about the only thing a skunk seems to ask as he stumbles across something is, "Can I swallow it?"

If one insect is good, a whole nest of them should be better —even if it's an underground swarm of yellow jackets. When the skunk comes across such a peppery bonanza, it has a field day. Tearing up the soil, it exposes the nest and its toothsome larvae. Heedless of the attacks of the adults, it proceeds to dine on every young yellow jacket it can find.

This is fine except for one small detail. The skunk leaves hundreds of angry adults behind. Thus things are put in a hostile state for the first passerby the next morning.

Farmers, woodsmen, and homeowners all over North America know the skunk, for the flat-footed creature is found from mid-Canada to Mexico. In the Midwest and South there's also the spotted skunk. This is a smaller, playful animal. It has the startling habit of standing on its front feet with its chemical warfare department raised high in the air. This may look funny, but it's best to laugh quietly—and at a distance.

Life gets under way for a new generation of the myopic little pacifists sometime in February or March, almost before the fitful winter sleep is over. The wandering male searches until he finds a female. They plight their troth with growls and chatterings and loving little snarls. This may take place in the female's wintering den, at the local refuse dump, or even under your front porch.

After mating, the male stays with his mate a few days longer. Then, with the nonchalance that's such a part of his whole attitude toward life, he ambles away some moonlit night, and goes to make another conquest.

But the female accepts her blighted romance as philosophically as she does almost everything else. She goes about her business as usual. Then, some nine weeks after her little love affair, she gives birth to four or five youngsters in a grass-lined nest underground.

About five weeks after they're born, the kits have developed striped fur coats. Now they're ready to see the world. They follow the mother skunk, single file, so close on each other's heels that a skunk family looks like a fat, piebald serpent wavering along at dusk.

When the mother stops suddenly to investigate a mouse nest, the youngsters may not get the message in time. Then they bump together like a train of freight cars. And if a misguided enemy attacks such a formation, it could well get the benefit of half a dozen riot guns in one withering blast.

From its first outing until late summer the family stays together. The youngsters tumble and play and growl their baby growls. In the process they also put on a layer of fat against the coming winter. They slowly turn into young adults at the expense of thousands of insects, hundreds of mice, snakes, frogs, and even a few eggs or chickens of some farmer. Thus by fall, when they go their separate ways, the nuclei of several potential skunk families dot the landscape.

Winter finds each skunk in a cubbyhole of its own choosing. This may or may not be with the consent of said cubbyhole's rightful occupant. Always the pacifists, skunks merely move in quietly. It matters little whether a woodchuck or marmot actually dug the hole and was there first. The skunk —often closely followed by half a dozen of his relatives who also stumble upon the same hole—just takes up residence. He expects no trouble and usually gets little beyond a few unprintable comments from the prior occupant who's forced to move over.

With a world of edibles beneath its nose and few enemies

that have the temerity to tackle it, why doesn't the skunk overrun North America? Actually, it does, in a moderate sort of way. The skunk—plus the chipmunk and the squirrel—is one of the few wild mammals still found living in many a city park. No matter where you live, there's probably a skunk less than a mile away.

There are effective curbs to its progress, however. Almost every dog, given the opportunity, has to learn about skunks the hard way. This is fine for subsequent wood pussies but may be rough on the first one it meets. And, of course, the dog's owner may finish the job. Then, too, the plodding little creatures come to grief by the thousands on the highways each year. Skunks have just never learned that not even they can bluff a car.

Least impressed by the skunk's artillery is the great horned owl. It doesn't give a hoot about all the musky odor in the world, for its sense of smell is almost nil. Spying that perfect black-and-white target in the dusk, it scoops it up and bears it triumphantly to its nest, trailing a scent that may linger in the trees for days. In fact, it's a rare nest of this bird that doesn't reek—especially when it rains and forgotten odors come to life again.

Foxes, too, occasionally practice their own way of outwitting the skunk. Rushing forward quickly, the nimble fox lures the skunk into firing. Dodging the spray, the fox repeats the process. Eventually, after eight or ten such feints, the skunk's supply runs out. Now it faces its tormentor with the only weapon left—its sharp but small teeth. This of course is a signal for the fox. It makes short work of the now defenseless skunk.

Then, too, there's the anti-skunk campaign that may be triggered when some overzealous child at camp bends down to pet the pretty kitty. And the discovery that a rare skunk may carry rabies sometimes is magnified senselessly—even though almost any mammal may also carry the disease, from bats to badgers, cows to chipmunks.

83

But for the most part *Mephitis mephitis* (which scientific name, given by tongue-in-cheek biologists, means "poison gas") makes a fine furry friend whether you enjoy yours from a safe distance in the yard at night or adopt one of the engaging critters made squirtless but forever dependent on you by the process of removing its tail guns.

There are pet stores that can supply you if you are interested. Or you can live on what to some people would seem the edge of disaster by inviting one of these undoctored putterers to share your home. I've done this twice and have been richly rewarded with the antics of the deadpan little entertainers. And I haven't had to bury any clothes, either.

However, for all their peaceful ways, the skunks insist on their right to have a mind of their own. So, if you take up housekeeping with one of the unexpurgated variety and something unforeseen *should* take place, I would ask one small favor:

Please, next time you talk to a skunk, don't mention my name.

The Four-Footed Nibblers

CHANCES ARE most gardeners have had unseen helpers this past summer—the mice, rabbits, and even deer that came uninvited to indulge in their own brand of pruning, thinning, and trimming. During the growing season, foliage covers their efforts. But when leaves fall, their mischief becomes apparent. And from now until spring no bit of plant tissue is safe from attack.

Meadow and pine mice nibble seed and fruit. Deer mice will even climb up into rosebushes or flowering crab apple trees for a snack. In winter, they creep about in runways beneath the snow line or in old plant litter and help themselves to the bark of trees or shrubs, often until the plant is completely girdled. Even trees eight inches in diameter may be attacked. Mice are one of the orchardist's chief problems, for their work is not apparent until spring thaws.

Roots and bulbs are not safe from mice, either. A friend once showed me a few iris rhizomes which had been eaten down through the crown until there was little left but a hollow shell. "I had them planted in rows," she said, "and the mice went right down the row."

There are several controls for these ground-level gremlins, but none is perfect. Orchardists often put a loose cylinder of quarter-inch mesh hardware cloth around the base of each young tree, embedding it about four inches deep and extending it two feet up the trunk. Although this is fine for flowering crabs, quinces, plums, and other single-stemmed plants, it's laborious and costs about fifteen cents per tree. Since mice often travel in ground litter, another method is to remove any excess not needed for mulching.

If neither of these methods gets results, traps and chemicals may have to be tried. Small wire-mesh live traps can be purchased at hardware stores. Set them out at dusk along a runway with a little bit of peanut butter, crackers, or oatmeal for bait. The next morning the occupant can be released unharmed in a vacant lot at least a mile away. Or the common snap-back traps can be used. They save a trip to the vacant lot.

Both mice and rabbits have sharp, gnawing front teeth. Mouse damage is usually confined to ground level or sheltered places. But if the upper tips of rose and raspberry bushes are cut off, rabbits are probably the culprits. They sit up, sometimes in broad daylight, and pull the tender shoots down to where they can nip them off with the peculiar slanting cut typical of the buck-tooth set.

Wire barriers around trees are effective against rabbits as well as mice. Larger box traps baited with carrot or apple can be used to catch them. Arasam, Z.I.P., and Ringwood repellent sprays can be applied to the bark of trees and shrubs.

If things get really out-of-hand, next year soybeans may be planted around the edge of the garden. The rabbits will devote their attention to the beans and leave other greenery alone. This is risky, however, for the rabbit may bring its family to enjoy the bonanza.

Until recently deer were not considered a garden pest. However, today in a number of states, it is almost impossible to grow vegetables without damaged and chewed-off plants. "The abandonment of farmland," a game warden told me, "has resulted in grown-over pastures and wasteland. This often makes prime deer territory, and if a garden is nearby, the deer will feed there too."

Another factor that accounts for deer prevalence is an apparent shift in the animals' habits. They used to browse on twigs and buds in the forest. Now they often come out in the open to graze on alfalfa and clover in a meadow.

Though it's quite well known that frayed twigs are typical of the feeding habits of deer, these large mammals may also produce another characteristic "sign." This is bark stripped along the trunk of a young tree. Chewing at poplar or apple bark, the deer may pull it up in ragged strips, breaking it off as high as it can reach.

Controlling deer can be a problem, for trapping and poisoning are obviously out. A three-foot fence will keep rabbits out of a garden but it takes eight or nine feet to deter a deer. The repellents used on rabbits can also be applied to tree bark and twig tips in autumn but they may render fruit and vegetables unfit to eat. Often the best thing is to clear away fence rows and overgrown areas adjacent to the garden.

The Terror of the Treetops

"THE ONLY fisher I ever saw was chasing a red squirrel in the treetops. It went through the branches after that chickaree like a big black ribbon. Picked off the squirrel in the third spruce."

My backwoods Vermont neighbor paused and eyed me as if daring me to question whether the nimble squirrel could be caught by an animal ten times its size. But I had heard enough about the "fisher-cat" to know this was not only possible but was a regular occurrence. Few animals of our northern forests are big, canny, or quick enough to escape the determined pursuit of this wily hunter.

It will run down a rabbit in fair chase. It can follow the pine marten—itself a destroyer of squirrels—to the treetops, where a breath-taking race occurs at top speed with the same final result. The fisher is North America's fastest tree-traveling mammal.

Despite its name, the fisher doesn't care to chase after fish. Although it is a good swimmer it prefers the salmon or dried smelt washed up with the debris along a lake shore.

Often called the black fox, black cat, or pennant's marten, the fisher is neither a fox nor a cat. It's a relative of the skunk and the wolverine. It has the weasel's inquisitive look, with a narrow face and small, rounded ears perked-up amid deep fur. About a yard from nose to tail-tip, with a dark, silky coat, it is low-slung, slender, catlike. Unlike cats, however, its claws cannot be retracted. Its magnificent tail, which makes up about a third of its length, is bushy like that of a fox.

An angry fisher is a terrible foe. Its tail lashes back and forth in rage. The sharp, curving claws dig into the ground or tree trunk as it tenses for battle. Its back arches like that of an outsized cat and with a hissing growl it flies at the enemy.

The size of the fisher's antagonist seems to make little difference to this lithe eight- to eighteen-pounder or its mate. If the animal is large, such as a raccoon or a fox, it may feint it out of position for a better advantage or throw caution aside and wade into direct combat. Preferring to run from a dog, it rarely comes out second if cornered; it can lick almost any kind of dog. Even the little weasel finds his darting reflexes no match for his larger cousin's blinding speed. His only hope for safety lies in a frantic dash for a mousehole. There is no authentic record of an unwounded fisher ever attacking a human being.

What the fisher seems to want most in this world is to be let alone. The Indians sometimes called him The Solitary One and told legends of his prowess. If there's another fisher in an area of less than eighty or one hundred square miles, one of them moves on to where it's not so crowded.

For all its individuality, the fisher is a creature of habit. Trappers know that it travels in a great circle through its territory, making the rounds to the same spot every few days. Every now and then it stops at certain old logs or stones on its course and solemnly deposits a musky secretion from special glands near the tail. These seem to serve as a communiqué to other fishers, especially during breeding season.

In March or April, there is a change in the attitude of these independent animals. The female, who has just given birth to the young which were conceived last year, leaves them while she goes to seek a mate. A whirlwind courtship and mating of perhaps a single encounter or just a few days begins the life of a new generation. She steals back to the babies she has just left, taking care not to let the male come near them, for he seems to have no qualms about consuming them on the spot.

Following this brief spring romance, the embryos within the mother go through a strange cycle. Instead of developing in normal fashion, they form several cells and remain, in suspended animation, until the following winter when they resume their growth. The result is one of the longest gestation periods known for mammals, equal to that of some whales and exceeding that of man—from eleven months to almost a year.

One to four, usually three, young are born the following year. Helpless and naked, blind for seven weeks, they are hidden in a hollow tree or stump. They depend completely on the periodic visits of their dark-furred mother, who remains closer to the den area during this period. In midsummer, though still small, they begin to hunt as a family group. As autumn approaches the youngsters drift off to establish territories of their own. They may catch a sleeping grouse in a fir tree at night or run down a snowshoe hare during the day.

The fisher is a moderate eater. Extra food is carefully stored, to be consumed on its next visit. Even nuts and fruits may be taken as an alternative when meat and fish are hard to come by.

The most unusual item of food—and one greatly relished, oddly enough—is an animal molested by few other creatures—the porcupine. The fisher makes quick work of the quill-pig by flipping him over and attacking his vulnerable underside. Or he may burrow under a porcupine in a snowdrift, coming up from below. The fisher may get a face full of quills for his trouble or he may pick up several dozen in his chest or forepaws during the fight. Strangely, these spines usually do little damage to him even when they work their way to the bone. They seem to localize without festering.

In some parts of the United States, the fisher has helped check the porcupine population.

Needful of a large individual territory and unable to compete with guns and traps, the fisher was for a while on the verge of extinction. Twenty years ago it was described as a vanishing species, on the downward trail with the American bison, the whooping crane, and the trumpeter swan. The fisher's demise was being hastened by the fact that its thick, lustrous dark fur sometimes commanded more than two hundred dollars for prime female pelts, making it one of our most valuable furs.

To save the fisher from extinction, the animal was given complete protection in the mid-thirties in Maine, New York, and New Hampshire. Also, a period of farm abandonment made more wild land available. More recently, the fisher fur market dropped and the skins fell to a tenth of their former value.

With the odds turned in his favor, he has begun to respond—but slowly. In fact, it is the fisher's low birth rate, plus his need for a large private territory, that probably prevented him from overrunning the woods in the first place.

No one can say yet how successful the campaign for his return will be. My friend Professor Malcolm Coulter of the Maine Cooperative Wildlife Research Unit, which has worked closely with this problem, points out that results at present are encouraging.

For a long time, people portrayed all predators as ruthless killers—"vermin" to be exterminated at any cost. But conservationists have learned through the years that you can't kill off one species without endangering the whole balance of nature, sometimes even throwing it out of gear.

Attempts have been made to raise fishers in captivity on a fur-farming basis. But these have not proved very profitable. Accustomed to the expanse and solitude of the forest, the fisher breeds with indifference in captivity, if at all. The female is nervous and edgy when her kits are born. An automobile backfire or a barking dog may make her rush to the box and kill them in a flash. In addition, she can be bred only over a two or three day period; if this time passes, she will not mate again until the following year.

Apparently the slow methods of natural reproduction plus trapping of fishers and reintroducing them to their old haunts seem to be the only means of restoring their rightful inheritance. With luck, the time may not be far distant when the "black cat" of the northwoods comes back to many of our northern states and Canada.

The Yard's a Stage for Squirrels

ALMOST EVERYONE has a member of the squirrel family for a neighbor. Even in the city the nearest park probably harbors a family of these engaging little mammals. They are so irrepressible they can get along almost anywhere.

Although the gray squirrel is a familiar creature, its far-flung clan is less well known. Not only do squirrels occupy most of North America but they have also gnawed out a niche for themselves everywhere from treetops to root level.

In the process of earning a living, the squirrels have often endeared themselves to their human neighbors. But just about as often their habits run afoul of man's best wishes.

A chipmunk may be the soul of cheerful industry as it nips the wings off maple seed pods and stores the seed in its cheek pouches. However, it is the soul of something else when it nips the heads off flowers, pilfers bulbs, and pokes holes in the lawn.

It is probably this mixture of good and bad which makes the squirrel tribe so interesting. There are times when not a friend can be found for the groundhog (also known as the woodchuck), which is the largest squirrel of them all. With what seems diabolical cleverness, it nibbles along a row of peas or peonies, scarcely leaving a plant untrimmed.

On the other hand, the groundhog's many underground burrows have served as convenient bolt-holes for small animals when pursued by predators or threatened by fire. And man has even set aside a special day in early February to honor the hoped-for awakening of this ten-pound waddling rodent.

It might seem at first that it would be difficult to tell the difference between squirrels and other rodents. All have those prominent gnawing incisors or buck teeth. However, if the rodent has a hairy or bushy tail, it is probably a squirrel —whether it be a ground-dwelling prairie dog, a flying squirrel, a western marmot, or a chipmunk.

It is among the tree squirrels, however, that the tail comes to its full glory. Not only does it serve as a stabilizer (somewhat like the feathers on an arrow) as the creature leaps from branch to branch, but it has other functions as well.

Sparky, a gray squirrel we have adopted, has shown me a few uses of the tail. Sparky was orphaned when tiny and was raised with a medicine dropper. When he doesn't want to be caught, he uses his tail just as a bullfighter uses his cape.

Flipping the great plumed appendage one way, he quickly darts the other. I have wondered about the abbreviated tail on an occasional squirrel, and now I think I know why. An enemy usually grabs at the most conspicuous portion—in this case the tail. All the predator gets is a handful of hair instead of a whole squirrel.

The eyes of the entire squirrel tribe are also adapted for survival. Since they have a host of enemies, squirrels must keep watch in all directions. Sparky's eyes are typical. Not only do they bulge, but they are set far to the sides of his head. Thus, he has what amounts to a panoramic view: to the front, both sides, up and down, and well to the rear. By contrast, our little fox terrier, as a typical predator, has eyes which peer forward so it can keep its prey in sight during the chase.

One of the hazards of living on the same premises with Sparky is the exuberance with which he greets us when we have been gone. We are welcomed with open "arms"—all four of them spread in a flying leap. Once the leap caught me full in the face and I bore the scratches for a week.

The common striped chipmunk seems to combine the characteristics of many squirrels into one active little body. Technically a ground squirrel, it is quite at home in the treetops. It occasionally falls, however, for it is not quite as sure-footed as a gray or red or fox squirrel.

Like most squirrels, the chipmunk is an inveterate hoarder. Popping up from its tunnel, it helps itself to almost any seed or fruit it can find. Internal cheek pouches allow it to stuff itself until it looks as if it had an outsize case of the mumps.

Popping out of sight again, it empties its hoard in an underground vault. Then it comes back up for more. I once found several quarts of cherry pits in a chipmunk nest accidentally unearthed by a bulldozer.

My Vermont neighbors tell me that the chipmunk's tail will tell what the winter will be like. If the tail is carried horizontally, to the rear, the winter will be mild. If it is carried aloft, like a jaunty flagpole, the winter will be normal, with fair amounts of snow and cold. But, if the tail is carried forward, watch out for a good old-fashioned blockbuster of a winter.

And how does the chipmunk react to its own predictions? It ignores them. In this it is like the woodchuck, the prairie dog, and most of its other ground squirrel relatives. It curls up in a tight little ball in a burrow well below the frost line and sleeps the winter through.

CREATURES
OF THE AIR

The Tidal Waifs

WHEN A perfectly good fleck of foam on the beach disappears after you've just been looking at it, it may have been a mirage. But when half a hundred such flecks take off in a graceful arc over the waves while you're staring right at them, that's more like a hallucination.

Of course they really aren't foam at all. Actually, they're a species of shore bird that gets along by looking just that way —or, if the light is right, by looking like nothing at all. For the sanderling, to use one of its many names, is an optical illusion with wings.

You'd think a bird roughly eight inches long and with a body nearly the size of a tennis ball would be conspicuous as it sits on the bare expanse of a beach at tide line. But not the sanderling. Instead of being shaded beneath and sun-struck above as a normal solid object would be, it's colored in just the opposite way: white below, rusty-mottled on top. So your eyes refuse to tell you it's a solid, living bird as it drowses on one foot, beak tucked under its wing. It seems to have about as much substance as the spindrift on the shore.

Even when the sanderling is in full flight you still get the impression that it's not really there. A band of the little birds wheels in precision just above the water, white wing patches flashing. Then, just as you start counting to see how many are in the flock, they all turn as of one mind—and their shadowy bodies disappear against the sparkle of the waves.

While you're still hopefully gazing out to sea, there's a movement just ahead of you on the beach—and there are your birds, alighting out of nowhere.

This is just the beginning. What happens next is equally surprising. Each bird in the flock runs to the brink of the swash left by the last wave and proceeds to follow it rapidly down the beach. Its black feet twinkle as it runs and its dark bill jabs the sand in a line as if it were the living needle of a sewing machine. Apparently heedless of the next gathering wave, the sanderling trots almost to the brink of disaster. Just in time it runs back—or flies, if it waited a second too long—ahead of the tumbling water. The instant the wave is spent, the sanderling turns and follows it down again, as if it were commissioned to poke holes in the entire beach. As one naturalist put it, "It follows the waves up and down like a little clockwork toy."

One time I was playing in the surf when I felt something wiggle beneath my toes. Scooping a handful of sand, I poked it apart as the water drained out of it. There was the cause of all the energy on the part of the feathered Yo-Yo: an olive-shaped creature known as the sand bug, plus several dozen of its tiny beach-flea relatives. Tough as seeds, these hardy little crustaceans live right in the zone of wave action. They float in the wild swash for a few seconds, searching out still lesser organisms on which to feed. As the water recedes, they burrow rapidly out of reach. Hence the sanderling must be quick to follow the wave or it will lose its meal.

That black bill isn't merely a pair of staccato forceps, however. Slightly opened as it's jabbed into the sand, it is marvelously sensitive, able to tell at once the difference between a bit of shell and a fleeing crustacean. If some potential bite proves to be uncooperative, the sanderling remains there, beak buried to the hilt, opening and closing its mouth in the sand. Finally it maneuvers its recalcitrant entree into a favorable position, gulps it down, and often quits the scene just a pinfeather ahead of tons of crashing water.

One August day I came across the body of a sanderling on a Cape Cod beach. Its sturdy inch-long beak was shaped like a long, blunt wedge. It had an almost leathery quality, related no doubt to its fingerlike sensitivity. Its feet were fashioned for their job, too. Since they patter over sand so wet that it appears the bird is walking on water, a hind toe would likely be a handicap; it would throw sand and water up against the little tidal waif's rump. So the hind toe was obligingly absent. The webless foot merely ended in a heel, somewhat like that of another famous runner, the ostrich.

The sanderling in my hand was remarkable in still another way. Although it was but a juvenile bird, it had most likely flown or run hundreds—maybe thousands—of miles in the few weeks of its existence. It was a long way from its arctic birthplace.

The parent birds, not yet mated and perhaps in separate flocks, quite likely passed north along this same beach in April or May. On the rising tide, when almost every wave successively covered more beach, they probably kept flying. When the tide turned, however, and the sand bars and flats began to emerge, the flock swooped in to eat, quite literally, on the run. Satiated, they'd come to a halt on the beach and stood there like so many bits of nothing until the waves or the weather drove them to flight again.

Day after day this pattern would continue. Whereas a robin, working north, might face bleak times as it looked for that early worm, the sanderling's food is as limitless as the sea itself. On good nights the flock might even travel after dark; I've seen them silhouetted against the moon over a New Hampshire shore and heard their single chirp of a call note above me in the night.

Some of the flock might turn west, stopping at marshes or ponds and finally appearing half a week later among the combers of the Great Lakes. Most, however, would continue north. New England, New Brunswick, Nova Scotia, Newfoundland, Labrador in turn would provide shore dinners for sanderlings and finally disappear astern. Only when they arrived at the bleak islands of the Arctic Ocean itself would the flock come to rest.

Now the males set up their territory. Lacking a winning song, they endeavor to woo their prospective mates with a low-altitude courtship flight, something like the dance of gnats over a stream. They rise about six feet off the ground and fly in a short line or slow circle. At the same time they utter a note which was described by a friend of mine who heard it as "a faint snarling, like a cat. Or maybe it was like the neighing of a tiny horse."

This aerial song-and-dance makes the point, however. The females, who at first appear so unconcerned that the males seem to be performing for each other, finally allow themselves to be persuaded as to the purpose of all these hundreds of miles to the frozen tundra. Each female chooses a spot in the middle of an arctic willow that grows almost flat on the ground, or she merely lines a depression in the earth with a few of last summer's leaves or catkins. Then she produces four light-olive, mottled eggs.

The arctic summer is fleeting. While humans far to the south leisurely open their vacation homes, life for the newly hatched sanderlings begins at top speed. Mid-June finds the chicks hatching. As each eggshell is discarded, the mother carries it away quickly before it reveals the nest to sharp-eyed ravens and the great piratical gull known as the skua. In this, as in brooding the eggs, she may be helped by the male. Within an hour after the last mottled chick has struggled free of its shell, the mother leads her family to the comparative safety of the pebbles and driftwood of the shore, which may be hundreds of feet away.

If an enemy threatens, the babies stop in their tracks. They blend into the landscape immediately. Then the mother goes through a whole gamut of tricks. Wings drooping, feathers puffed, stumbling, she draws attention to herself. Making short flights, she flaunts those conspicuous white wing patches. Calling her little "chip" or a soft, snarling note, she offers herself as a tempting target.

This fools many a predator, but not the arctic fox. Seeing such an elaborate display, the fox circles carefully, searching out the motionless morsels with its keen nose. If successful, it may take the entire brood, leaving the mother guarding an empty beach.

The chicks that escape grow at an astonishing speed. Two weeks after they stole furtively from the nest, they can fly. Nor is it any too soon. Their short summer is closing.

Joining with other groups, they travel south, sometimes hitting our beaches as early as late July. Often the earliest arrivals meet and chase the waves with laggards who never made it beyond the same spot in the spring. Thus at a casual glance it would seem as if the same sanderlings had been there all summer. But the adolescents in their pepper-and-salt instead of the cinnamon-and-sugar top coloring of the adults are relatively easy to identify. And since a few birds may choose to spend the rest of the year on the New England coast, the sanderling seems almost like a resident bird instead of the continental traveler it really is.

Actually, "global traveler" is more like it. While some of "our" sanderlings may stay here, most of them go on and on. Down the coast they travel, pausing long enough on North Carolina's Outer Banks for me to get a picture of a flock at Hatteras on August 8—merely teen-agers and already two thousand miles from home. Soon those same little birds would delight watchers at Myrtle Beach, South Carolina, then Fort Lauderdale, then Miami. A similar migration takes place on the Pacific coast.

Still headed south, the sanderling flies into Mexico, where it becomes *el Charlito blanco*. On it goes to Panama, Brazil —perhaps all the way to Patagonia, which sounds impossibly south—and is, clear at the tip of South America.

Our familiar beachcomber repeats the story, with variations, over much of the world. In the process it gathers a host of names. Along the water's edge in Scotland, I caught that familiar flash of white as a band of "peeps" wheeled away in alarm. My brother in Hawaii sees the little "hune-kai" or "sea foam" on the white sand beaches of the Kona Coast.

"It's been seen on the black sands, too," he wrote to me, "but not very often. No wonder—it must stand out like a flashlight."

In Australia, the "wick" belongs to the Land Down Under as much as the kookaburra, the honey eater, and the hoopoe. Along African shores it is the "surf-bird," while in scientific jargon everywhere this cosmopolitan globe-trotter is known as *Crocethia alba*, which means, sensibly enough, "the white sandpiper."

So if, for some strange reason, you elect to swap our own shores for a tropical island somewhere, *all* the scenery may not be new. Chances are you'll be greeted by the familiar foam-colored little riveter, which companionably makes room for you in the land of the sanderling.

The Ph.D. with Feathers

CROWS ARE like that. You never know what they're going to do next. I first learned this from a two-pound rascal who supposedly answered to the name of Inky. A friend of mine let me take him while he was away at camp for a couple of weeks.

The first few days were fine. Inky shared the barn with our cow and made himself at home in the rafters over the stall at night. When we fed him, he'd dunk the hard crusts in his water to soften them. If he spotted anybody in the yard, he'd fly down to light on that person's shoulder. Then he'd peck companionably at a tidbit or whatever else was available: a ring or a button or a flower design on a blouse.

The next few days weren't so fine. One morning he landed on Mrs. Wheeler when she came to visit. To her surprise—and probably to his, too—the brooch fell off her sweater when he whacked at it. So he dropped down, scooped up his prize, and bore it triumphantly to the barn while we watched in anguish. He was back before I could find where he'd hidden it.

The next to go was my genuine simulated pearl-handled knife. I'd won it by selling three dozen tins of salve—mostly to my parents, who probably have some of the stuff to this day. Then my sister lost her wristwatch. So there was no choice but to put a ladder up and search for the whole business in the rafters.

When he squared off and took a crack at the gold pivot

tooth of a traveling salesman, however, I made up my mind: if all this could happen in two weeks, my first crow was going to be my last.

That was some thirty years ago. Since then, although as a naturalist I've had my share of dozens of waifs and orphans that have been turned over to me for safe-keeping, I've never gone back on my resolve. Occasionally, in the parade of creatures brought to my door, I spot one of the innocent-looking black rascals. I may keep him overnight, but seldom longer. Usually there's some lucky person who wants him.

One of my favorites in this little game of passing the buck is a good-natured lady who lives on a farm a few miles from my Vermont home. She shares her abode with approximately ten descendants, a score of cats, dogs, and chickens, and one of my crows. Actually, I think I've sent her three of the birds but she's learned to pass the buck, too.

It's fun to visit her just to sit back and absorb it all. She tells me about the lamb that slept with some of the children while it was sick, the pony that liked root beer, and the pigeon who stayed in the kitchen all winter to keep warm. And while we're talking, Sammy crow is eyeing the buckle on my camera strap or investigating my shoelaces.

"That crow follows us everywhere," she told me on one of my visits. "Not only around the house but he flies over the kids on their bicycles, too. He even tags after us down to the store."

I considered this one for a moment. The store was two miles away. Did she mean that he followed the car?

"Oh, sure," Mrs. Brown said. "We have to put him in the shed when we're really going away or he'd follow us clear to Montpelier. But when we go to the store, he flies about twenty feet above the car all the way—if we don't go faster than twenty-five miles per hour. That's about his top speed. On the way back, though, he goes cross-country. Beats us home every time."

She recounted some of Sammy's other activities. She told me how he'd sit on a low limb until the cat was asleep, fly down, and steal food out of her dish—and then peck her tail when he was through. He'd learned to imitate the crying of the current youngest member of the family, too—"so real that I want to put diapers on him," she said.

During one of my visits, Sammy demonstrated that he'd learned to talk as well. Mrs. Brown was proud of his accomplishment. Of course, she assured me, they hadn't tried to split his tongue in the ancient belief that it would improve his speech.

His speech did need improving, however. Although his vocabulary was limited, it would have made a seagoing parrot blush. Mrs. Brown, naturally, was certain that he must have learned those words in town.

He was a kleptomaniac, too, just like that crow of my childhood. Mrs. Brown pointed to something in the top of a tall maple tree. "Those are Benjamin's sunglasses," she told me while I dutifully squinted skyward. "That crow took them up there and got them caught in the fork of a branch. They've been there ever since last month."

Most of the bright objects spirited away by Sammy, however, ended up in a hollow stump in the backyard. "We've found jar covers, ballpoint pens, spoons, chewing gum wrappers, and half of Rosemary's bottle cap collection in that stump," she said. "One time we even found a quarter. So when we're missing something, we just send one of the kids out to look in Sammy's collection. Like as not, that's where it is."

The perpetrator of these deeds comes by it naturally. His audacious family, which includes magpies, jays, and ravens, has always had to live by its wits. Fate, tongue-in-cheek, has handed the magpies and jays a color pattern about as subdued as a clown costume. It has cloaked the crow and its larger raven cousins in a glistening steely black. Thus attired, the conspicuous creatures have had to rely on their brains—and brass—to make their way in the world.

A new generation of *Corvus brachyrhynchos*—roughly translated, "the black bird with the short beak"—gets under way in late February in our southern states, or in mid-April as far north as Canada. During the winter, while crows have been assembled in great flocks near cornfields, in winter beeches, and along river beds, they've fraternized impartially with members of either sex. Then, as they work their way back to the uplands of their summer abode, they begin to take a new interest in each other.

Courtship among crows is an impressive affair. Crow chases crow, shouting a guttural version of sweet nothings. As it flies, it attempts everything from wing-whistling dives to sudden straight-up stalls in the air. Often several birds get in on the fun at once. A flock of romantic crows may look like some strange airborne squadron of windswept leaves.

Ornithologists say it's almost impossible to tell females from males by sight alone. Apparently this confuses the crows, too, at times. A male may press his attentions on another male until he is set straight by the outraged second party. Or half a dozen males may chase a single female while leaving other, apparently desirable, females to preen their feathers alone. "But," as one lady ornithologist informed me with a sigh, "that's the way it is sometimes, I guess."

Finally all cases of mistaken identity are cleared up. Now comes the next stage. Crows prefer to nest in tall evergreens with a commanding view of the surrounding forest. But such trees are often at a premium. So a single tree may receive the attentions of half a dozen pairs of crows at once.

In the process of winnowing it down to one or two nests per tree, family lines may become a trifle blurred. Not only does one set of crows pilfer twigs from the nest of neighbors, but an enterprising male may even pilfer an extra mate. Occasionally such a lady has even been known to share nesting duties with the rightful homeowner. Wife No. 1, apparently seeing how things are, moves over philosophically and makes room for No. 2.

The nest itself looks like a brushpile. It may be larger than a dishpan in order to accommodate some twenty inches of brooding crow. Its ramshackle appearance belies its sturdy construction. Crows may use the same nest year after year. All that's necessary for spring housecleaning each year is a few more twigs and a new lining of grass or leaves.

The eggs are produced in late April or May. Four or five in number, they are half the size of a hen's egg, greenish and blotched with brown. The female may begin to sit on the nest as soon as the first egg is laid. Thus her family may be spaced several days apart. Now her mate takes over the food-gathering chores.

Parent crows are models of good behavior around the nest. Whatever their failings elsewhere, they alight silently in a nearby tree and steal home quietly without bothering anybody. They may even allow lesser birds to build nearby. Ordinarily the eggs and fledglings of these smaller neighbors would be fair game for hungry crows; however, the little birds may not be interfered with at all. Perhaps they serve as camouflage for the crows, whose eggs and young may themselves be in danger from raccoons, red squirrels, and the nocturnal visits of the great horned owl.

After about three weeks the crowlets struggle into the world. Blind and naked except for a scant covering of gray down, they're helpless and silent at first. The parents begin a ceaseless shuttle-run of food to the frantically growing youngsters, who may put away more than their own weight in nutrients every day.

Then one morning the quiet forest is shocked as the first youngster proclaims his advanced status. In another day or so his two or three littermates have found their voices, too. Shouting insistently, they make a sound like "car, car," instead of the "caw, caw" of the mature birds.

It's often at this noisy stage that they're captured and borne happily home by farm boys for the delight and despair of some fortunate family. But, barring such an event, the little fellows spend about a month in the nest at the expense of almost every conceivable kind of insect, mollusk, frog, mouse, fruit, and vegetable air-lifted to them by the parents. Then one day in late June or July, the new crows launch themselves on an unprotected world.

From then until some hazard of life catches up with him seven or eight years later, the crow goes his nefarious way. Such are the pranks and services he performs that he's soundly praised or roundly cussed by his human neighbors— all depending on what he was last doing when somebody saw him.

The farmer plants his corn for the third time and shakes his fist at a nonchalant sentry crow in a tree just out of gun-shot range. The camper watches approvingly through binoculars as a pair of the black avengers thrashes the life out of a timber rattlesnake. The hunter rejoices as he learns that the crow's six hundred known items of food include the young of the snapping turtle; there'll be fewer ducklings pulled under the water if there are fewer snappers, he figures. But then that hunter waxes poetic with wrath as he comes across a duck's nest ruined by the same crow.

Through it all, the crow follows his checkered career with happy impartiality. Spotting a hawk or owl in a tree, he shouts an excited summons. Soon every crow within hearing arrives to drive the unfortunate creature out of the area. Often the din attracts more distant crows, who pick up the fleeing owl where the first mob leaves off.

This, of course, reflects no concern on the part of the crow for the owl's potential threat to any of its smaller neighbors. Having routed the common enemy, the crow may exact a toll—in the form of a baby bird—on its triumphant way home. I saw one crow tweak off entirely a small branch which held a vireo's nest. Then, carrying the whole affair, it flew over the landscape, trailed by the distraught parents.

Such antics have brought the crow under the malediction of man for centuries. Almost without let-up, the crow has found a price on his head since the days of the Revolutionary War. One of the first laws enacted in New York State was to offer a reward for dead crows. Harried officials have paid as much as twenty-five cents each for crows offered by hunters. Irate farmers have paid fifty cents and more for every crow surrendered to them when sprouted corn plants were at their tenderest. Vindictive gunners have risked life and limb to set a stuffed owl up in a tree. Then, retiring to some hidden spot, they've waited to give the black bandits their comeuppance.

Organized "crow shoots" have netted fantastic numbers of the birds in a single blast. During the nonbreeding season especially, crows band into huge flocks for roosting, togetherness, and general pandemonium. A grove of trees may be black with their hulking forms as thousands settle down for the night. Charges of dynamite or a posse of hidden gunmen armed to the teeth may do them in before they know what has happened. One such vendetta near Rockford, Illinois, laid low almost a third of a million crows.

Despite all this unflattering attention, the crow has apparently never had it so good. There are probably as many of them as ever; some wildlife experts say they are at an all-time high right now. Without a single law passed in its favor, the crow yet benefits by another man-made condition: the cutting of the great forests and the opening of the land for cultivation.

Deep woods are fine for nesting, it seems, but the shadowy forest floor provides slim pickings for food. Its quiet carpet of humus presents few edibles—even for a crow's digestion, which is about as finicky as a cement mixer. Cornfields and fence rows and farmlands, however, are another matter. Abandoned farms growing up to weeds produce such delicacies as poison ivy berries and the more prosaic fruits and insects. So Inky and his kin find things to their liking in every one of the states in the continental United States, most of Canada, and down into Mexico.

Able to spot with unnerving accuracy the difference between a man with a stick and a man with a gun, they haunt the farms and suburbs and often make their way to the city dump. In fact, nearly every metropolitan area has its crows —as if they knew the ordinance against firearms within city limits.

At that, these animated bullseyes take no chances. They usually post a sentry before they swoop down to pick at a dead animal or a bit of litter along a roadside. And they keep bankers' hours, too. When day breaks, they talk among themselves for some time, almost as if deciding whether it's worth it or not to get up. A. C. Bent's incomparable *Life Histories of American Birds* points out that as many as two dozen other species may be active before the crows finally get around to leaving the roost. And they retire early; long processions of crows headed for the roosting grounds may be seen from mid-afternoon until dusk.

"If men could bear feathers and be provided with wings," Henry Ward Beecher once said, "very few would be clever enough to be crows." When biologists learn that a crow is able to run a simple maze and tell the difference between a hole with a square opening and one with a round opening, they generally agree that here indeed is a mental giant among birds.

This "feathered Ph.D.," as he's been called, is apt to come up with a new trick at any moment. At the beach I've seen him carry a clam to a height above the road and drop it to the concrete below. Then he swoops down for a feast on the shattered clam. Two crows may attack a bird's nest—one getting the parents to chase it while the other moves in for a meal of eggs or young. And one crow I heard of used to delight in "riding" the crossarms of revolving TV antennas in a neighborhood, hopping up as each one came around and playing general hob with the picture.

Of course the familiar scarecrow with its stiff arms and floppy clothes doesn't fool any wild crow worth the name. Nor do such gadgets as TV dinner trays strung around a corn patch to bang and flutter in the wind. Neither does the startling sight of a dead crow or two hung by its legs in a field "to teach the rascals a lesson." To a creature which lives by keen eyes and keener wits, such apparitions just don't make much sense.

This last year, however, a friend of mine may have stumbled on a way to narrow the credibility gap. "My son Carl was flying his kite," he recalled. "He was using his fishline for string and had the whole works rigged to his pole. But he'd forgotten to tie the string to the spool. When the kite hit the end of the line, it kept right on going.

"Of course it fell to earth as soon as there was no tension on the string," he continued. "By the time my boy was able to rescue it, the line was strung all over—trees, bushes, a couple of loops across a corner of one of my fields. So Carl just took the kite and left the line right there. And, do you know, all summer long the crows stayed out of that corner of the cornfield. They must have figured that skinny little thread was some new kind of trap."

My neighbor plans to string more thin line this year to see if it will work a second time. However, when I expressed an interest in it and told him I was writing this article, he insisted that I not give his name.

"Why?" I asked. "So your neighbors won't laugh at you?"

"Heck, no," he said. "It's not that I mind the neighbors. It's just that the danged crows might read the story and find out it's all a fake."

And he just *could* be right, after all. Crows are like that.

Bluebird

WHEN YOU see a bluebird, you can understand the Indian legend that the soft-voiced little creature was originally a portion of the summer sky. According to the legend, the Great Spirit breathed life into a fragment of the heavens and sent it north on the heels of winter as a promise of returning spring.

This sparrow-sized bird with the incredibly blue back and the reddish-orange breast first sings his warbling song over my Vermont meadows about the first week in April. The occasion of his arrival is a real treat. My whole family turns out to see him. Shortly thereafter his mate joins him. She wears the same colors, but in subdued tones.

The pair may spend as much as a month house-hunting or may settle down to a chosen site within a week or two. And two years ago I had the immense satisfaction of hastily putting up a nest box while the male was singing in the yard and having him alight on its roof before I got back into the house. He raised a family in it, too.

Lucky is the gardener who can claim a nesting pair of bluebirds. From the moment they appear until the four or five young are fledged in early summer they watch continuously for insects. While a warbler or chickadee will search every twig and crevice of bark and a robin runs over the lawn, a bluebird has a way of feeding that's unique. In fact, it's so characteristic that you can identify a distant bluebird by its actions long before you can spot its colors.

Perching quietly on a wire or dead limb, the bluebird watches the ground below. If an insect moves, down drops the bird, picks it up, and returns to the same perch. It may do this again and again, occasionally snatching passing insects from the air as well. No other bird behaves in quite this way.

We've been fortunate in having bluebirds around our garden almost every year. They take an astonishing number of insects. While the female incubates the eggs, the male may call his liquid warble from the top of a craggy tree. He's alert to what's happening on the ground, however, and swoops down at intervals in his characteristic fashion. Good husband that he is, he may present a tidbit to his mate or take turns on the eggs himself.

It's easy to tell when the eggs have hatched. The activities of the parents increase tremendously. Both birds scour the area within a couple of hundred feet in all directions for potential food. They're so clever at catching insects that they can pick up a fly or beetle, hold it in the beak, and snap up another without losing the first.

One time I checked the frequency of their visits; every two and one-half minutes one parent or the other fed the babies. A little arithmetic told me that even with only a single insect per visit this meant that some 288 insects met their doom in a twelve-hour day—to say nothing of what the parents themselves ate. And I'm sure this is a conservative estimate for many baby birds may consume their own weight or more in food each day. Then, too, I've seen the birds arrive at the nest with their beaks crammed full of insects.

To look at the bluebird, you'd hardly suspect it to be a close cousin of the robin. And it seems even less likely, from appearance at least, that both are members of the thrush family—that celebrated group which includes the hermit thrush, the wood thrush, and the nightingale. But young bluebirds, and young robins, too, clearly belong in the thrush family, with their speckled breasts and somber plumage.

Even here the glorious blue of the bluebird is promised in just a hint of color among the flight feathers.

Much as it is admired by nearly all who have made its acquaintance, the bluebird finds itself unwittingly turned away by those who love it best. For our modern methods of gardening and farming leave little room for the winsome creature to make a living. Gone is the old apple orchard with its knotted trees and hollow stubs that served as both food and nesting sites for bluebirds. In its place are closely pruned trees kept in peak condition by powerful spray rigs. The wooden fencepost with its "bob-wire," as my Vermont neighbors call it, no longer presents a decaying knothole for the bird to use. Instead it's replaced by skinny metal posts and a single strand of electric wire. And since electric fences are easy to move around, the overgrown fence row with its myriads of potential bluebird spots is gone, too.

Add to this two other threats. These are the starling and the English sparrow, both of which like to nest in the very sites preferred by the bluebird. And in competition with either, the peaceful bluebird quickly loses.

Happily, the picture for *Sialia sialis* isn't entirely bleak. In fact, it could easily be changed. Since housing is the big problem confronting the bluebird, a little effort can yield heartening results. A single nest box of proper size and location may make all the difference. But note carefully those words "proper size and location." Just a "bird box" put up anywhere will probably not do at all.

Internal dimensions of a bluebird house should provide a cavity at least 4½ inches square and 9 inches deep. Drill at least six ¼-inch holes near the top to let out summer's heat and four in the bottom to allow moisture from driving rains to escape. Use old, unpainted wood if possible. Construct the roof or one panel so that it can be removed for cleaning in spring.

You must pay most attention to the front of the box with its entrance hole. Make the hole no larger than 1½ inches;

this will keep out the larger starling. The top of the hole should be no less than 2 inches from the roof.

The box may be made of wood 1 inch thick or more for strength, but the front should be ½ inch thick or even less. This allows the bird to go in and out more easily than it could through a hole in a thicker board. And the inside should be rough so the youngsters can climb up when it comes time to fly. Don't put a peg or perch of any kind on the outside.

Just as important as construction is the spot you choose to erect your birdhouse. While the bluebird is not terribly fussy as to height aboveground or nearness to human habitation, the English sparrow is more choosy. If you're careful, you can put the box where the sparrows would prefer not to use it.

English sparrows would rather nest fairly well above the ground but a bluebird will often nest in a box as low as chest level. English sparrows nest near or about buildings, while the bluebird can get along perfectly well out in the open. Therefore, put your nest box on a single post about 4 to 6 feet high and well away from the nearest building—100 feet, if space permits.

Peace-loving as the bluebird is, it requires elbow room as far as its own species is concerned. If boxes are much closer than 400 feet, probably only one will ever contain bluebirds. So putting up two or three in your backyard may increase the odds of getting a single family, but that's about all.

Sometimes it's possible to put nest boxes at 400-foot intervals along the edge of a meadow or in adjacent lots, thereby establishing a "bluebird trail." Lots of the boxes may go begging the first year or may attract wrens, chickadees, tree swallows, and the like. But if you're lucky, there'll be an occasional bluebird. Then the insects will have reason to quit the area for good while your eyes and your ears delight in the return of "the bird that carries the summer sky on its back."

Birds' Nests

WHEN THE birds reappear this spring, a number of them will be merely passing through. It would be useless to try to detain them. Many warblers, for instance, are on their way to join the juncos, tree and fox sparrows, and evening grosbeaks that desert the winter feeder for more northern nesting sites.

Other new arrivals, however, will take their places here with the chickadees, cardinals, nuthatches, woodpeckers—plus those persistent starlings and house sparrows—as they find a spot to raise their young. Each will build its own special style of home.

Your visitors have three basic needs: food, shelter, and territory. Summer food is seldom a problem, except when the youngsters are practically exploding with growth. Then the parents must work continuously to feed them. Shelter—including a place for the nest—and territory are so important that if either is missing a bird may not remain.

Scarcely three dozen American species use birdhouses, even when available. The vital nesting need may be for a tuft of grass, a low shrub, a fork of a tree, a ledge beneath the eaves, or even the corner of a flat roof.

The ground-nesting song sparrow builds at the base of a grass clump. Savanna sparrows have a similar nest, but roofed over, so it's hard to find. Upright reeds pulled together support the redwing's woven bowl. Ovenbirds get their name from their nests: a cubbyhole hidden under the leaves and humus of the forest floor.

Ground-nesting birds may lose a family to a marauding skunk or shrew but like most other birds they quickly begin a second one—or a third or fourth. Bobolinks and meadowlarks, though, with their first nest destroyed by haying, may lose the next home when the second cut is made.

Probably as many nests are found in shrubs as in any other location. This can easily be noted before the leaves appear for the summer. Last year's nests are plainly visible. Their twigs, grass, and fibers are expertly fitted into a crotch and anchored there with a few strands woven around the branches. Cardinals, catbirds, mocking birds, finches, warblers, thrushes, and many kinds of sparrow make their homes in shrubbery.

Almost anything may go into a nest. The chipping sparrow formerly lined its home with horsehair. Now, in this mechanized age, it uses fibrous plant roots or even the shed hairs from a pet collie or Persian cat. Our two horses change their coats twice a year; we may discover their long tail hairs later, wound around and around in a chipping sparrow's nest. A goldfinch nest brought to me by a friend was incredibly soft with thistledown and dandelion fluff. Last summer a wood thrush nested in a rhododendron in a New Jersey suburban park. Its nest had the usual twigs and mud—with the added fillip of a full-sized piece of facial tissue. This remained, a status symbol, until the first pelting rain.

Social climbing reaches its peak with the cowbirds. The female lays her egg in the nest of a smaller bird, which dutifully raises the blatant stepchild as its own. But sometimes the scheme backfires. Yellow warblers or chipping sparrows, two frequent victims, may build a whole new nest right on top of the offending egg.

Except for crows, eagles, and large hawks, few birds build

their nests in the very tops of trees. Many birds do make their homes on the limbs or among the twigs. The hanging pouch of the Baltimore oriole is suspended from a few slender twigs with nothing but air between it and the ground far below. Using string, plant fibers, and shreds of bark, the bird has only its beak to make a structure which may be used for several seasons. The nests of vireos, like dainty bowls, hang from forked twigs. Blue jays make a bulky nest of twigs, lined with grasses. Sometimes they'll add a shiny bit of tinfoil or a piece of broken glass. For all their brashness, jays are silent around the nest and often sneak to it by hopping from one branch to another. The exquisite hummingbird's nest, of plant down and spider web, is stuccoed with lichens and placed right on a limb.

The robin's nest, so often found in the crotch of a tree or along a limb, is of grass and fibers, plus a generous supply of mud. A female robin is a disreputable sight after she has carried the mud tucked under her chin and then shaped it to fit by pressing it in place with her breast. Robins are individualists when choosing a location for their nests. They may build under the eaves of a porch, on the girders of a bridge, or in the back seat of an abandoned car. And, like a woman rearranging the furniture, they may build several adobe homes before they get one they like.

Mud is used by other birds, too. Barn swallows plaster their mud nests against the splintery rafters of my barn. Cliff swallows build their crockery jugs beneath the eaves on the outside, and a pair of phoebes makes a fine concoction of mud, feathers, and grass up in one corner of our back porch. We bow to their version of beauty, since they are wonderful flycatchers.

Chimney swifts formerly nested in hollow trees. Now they usually nest in chimneys, with or without a fire below. The nest, made of twigs, is cemented together and stuck to the side of the chimney with saliva. Apparently all that smoke and soot just hardens the nest in place and makes it cozy for

the youngsters. A Chinese relative of the swift supplies the
pièce de resistance for bird's-nest soup.

Other occupants of hollow trees include woodpeckers and
flickers, which usually excavate their own holes. The following year a hole may be used by a titmouse or chickadee,
whose sturdy black beak may redesign the hole to its own liking. The bluebird may use it a third year, sometimes coming
to grief as a house sparrow or starling moves in despite its
frantic protests.

Increasing numbers of people feed birds the year round. A
woman I know feeds chickadees from her hand and lips.
One May day a chickadee flew from its nest hole, landed on
her chin, took careful aim—and tweaked a hair out of her
head.

If you put out bits of string for nesting birds, keep them
short. Otherwise the birds may strangle themselves. A friend
of mine put out a long piece of grocery string. Three cedar
waxwings tried to take it away—in three different directions.

Tree swallows will appreciate fluffy white feathers as
building material. You can tack wooden ledges and shelves
under eaves and porches. Common pigeons may use such
places or may make a sketchy nest right on a deep windowsill or a flat roof.

Nest boxes work best for the hole-nesting species. A hole
just a shade under 1½ inches is perfect for bluebirds but
will keep out starlings. Purple martins prefer to nest in
"apartment houses" of many units. A birdhouse can be made
of any color but a neutral color may be preferred to glaring
white. And dark colors absorb too much heat on a summer
day. A nest box should be ventilated and its interior rough-
ened so the fledglings can clamber up to the exit hole.

Sometimes birds aren't one bit fussy as to housing. I know
of a bluebird that built a nest in the pocket of some abandoned overalls. A pair of English sparrows raised a brood in
the mouth of a fire siren—daily noon blasts and all. And a

close friend had to forego water skiing for three weeks until a family of mourning doves moved out of the prow of his boat.

Then there's the question of territory, especially among members of the same species. Ten bluebird houses in an acre of backyard won't mean ten bluebird families. You might get one bluebird and nine tree swallows. Each species has its own need for private territory. Swallows and martins can live almost wing-to-wing. Bluebird boxes should be four to five hundred feet apart. Robins get along with perhaps half that distance, the males patrolling the boundaries and often fighting where they join, just to keep everybody honest. Many birds proclaim their own territory with song—the avian equivalent of "The Smiths live here" on a lawn signpost.

A few birds want more than their share. I've seen a kingbird drive a song sparrow right to the ground, far from the tyrant flycatcher's nest. The house wren, one of our smallest birds, nests in holes. Not only does he proclaim his bailiwick with incessant song but he goes even further. Picking up twigs as quickly as possible, he will even try to sing with his mouth full. Then, patrolling the backyard with his twigs, he'll plug every hole in sight.

CREATURES
OF THE WATER

A Half-Ton of Mermaid

COLUMBUS WAS the first white man to see her. She lolled in the coastal waters of Haiti. Like the sirens pictured on his maps, she seemed to be half-woman, half-fish. After a good look the sailors turned away. And well they might. For now we know that their "mermaids" were really slow, pudgy mammals known as manatees. Columbus, probably still believing they were aquatic ladies, was kind: "They were not as beautiful as they had been painted," wrote the explorer gallantly. The big gray manatee is roughly the shape of a short, fat cigar. The bald head widens into the body without neck or shoulders. The caressing arms of the sailor's dreams are just leathery little paddles. The rounded tail looks as if it belonged to a giant beaver. And it sports a wheat-stubble mustache on a bulbous harelip. Yet there's little doubt that manatees have kept the mermaid story going for centuries. They're like humans in many ways.

They kiss each other or throw a neighborly flipper over the back of a companion. They're warm-blooded and breathe two or three breaths at five- to ten-minute intervals. The babies nurse from a pair of teats located in the chest region. They may even ride piggy-back on mother like a papoose.

It was the West Indian manatee that Columbus discovered. A twin-sister form, the Florida manatee, lives along the Florida coast. Two other species are found in the Amazon region and in West Africa.

A king-sized Florida manatee may tip the scales at one thousand five hundred pounds. Nearly fifteen feet from stem to stern, it may be a matronly seven feet around the middle. Average ones are about half this size. They are plump and smooth, like sausage, with a skin two inches thick, sometimes covered with sea moss and barnacles. Two little eyes peer out through browless skin. Pencil-point holes behind them are the only signs of ears.

The manatee seeks only to live at dreamy peace with its world. Hanging in the water with head and tail drooping, it couldn't fight if it wanted to. The only teeth it has are molars for grinding weeds. It has no claws, just three little flat fingernails. It has no hind legs with which to kick. Seemingly voiceless, it cannot bellow or growl. It relies on size and seclusion for safety.

When not feeding during the day, it hides in the bottom of a turbid, brackish river. Every five to ten minutes it slowly comes up to breathe. Then it slowly drifts to the bottom like a water-soaked log.

The first scientist to dissect a manatee must have been surprised at the ivorylike density of the bones. Some have theorized that this most likely helps the manatee to sink easily to the bottom. Yet it's delicately balanced. It can rise slowly, sink, or stop at any depth without perceptible effort. Biologists are still puzzled as to the exact way it's done.

The shy creature feeds mostly at night, scooping grass and weeds toward its mouth. Then its bristly harelip takes over. The right and left halves work like the jaws of a pair of pliers. They grip the food, pull it loose, and tuck it down into the mouth, as much as one hundred pounds in a night.

A few manatees in a submarine pasture eat with such gusto that on a still night they can be heard an eighth of a mile away. But it's hard to sneak up on them. Despite those tiny ear-holes, manatees detect the slightest sound. Big as it is, the manatee is a master at camouflage. The sea moss patches on its back blend it with the bay bottom. And it throws up a smoke screen of mud and silt when feeding that may linger in the water for hours.

The love life of our mermaid is only partially known. Her prospective suitor may feel the urge to go courting at nearly any time of the year. He nuzzles her with a few bristly kisses while she drowses in the water. Then he snuggles up to her and puts an affectionate flipper over her back. If she's not interested, she moves unhurriedly away. Then he sometimes does a sedate barrel-roll. This is his way of trying to show he didn't really care.

Mating probably takes place at the surface. The new baby arrives after five-and-one-half months. The little fellow may be about three feet long, weighing perhaps fifty pounds. With only the water for a cradle and because he needs to surface for air, he must swim as soon as he is born. He valiantly dog-paddles with his flippers, keeping near his solicitous mother. It's several days before he learns to use his tail in the up-and-down motion which serves him the rest of his life.

Like any other mammal, he is nourished with his mother's milk. But she doesn't hold him up above the water to nurse, charming though the picture would be. She just hangs suspended underwater or grazes along the bottom. He feeds as best he can, bobbing up every minute or so for air. He may nurse for a year or longer, striking out on his own when he's about two years old.

He and his mother keep pretty much to themselves. If they become separated, he welcomes her back with a whiskery kiss. If danger threatens, he takes shelter beneath her bulk.

Sometimes the protective impulse of the mother results in tragedy for her baby. Completely helpless on land, she is unable even to hunch along like a seal if stranded. If caught in an ebbing tide, she would surely try to protect him by the only method she knows. As the water lowered, she would cover him with her huge, sagging body. When the tide returned, it would be too late. The life of her youngster would have been snuffed out.

A manatee in an aquarium often lies on the bottom, like a sunken canoe. Visitors sometimes fail to recognize it as an animal and ask the attendant where the tank's occupant is supposed to be. They are astonished when the big creature lazes up to the surface for a breath of air. Even when the tank is drained it keeps breathing at the same five- to ten-minute intervals.

When manatees play, they work up quite a commotion. The great tails whack the water and they nuzzle and bump each other. They roll over and over like a barrel. They come up beneath a neighbor, half lifting it out of the water. Strangely, it's nearly always the adults that play. The sober little babies keep close to their mothers.

Shy as it is, the manatee is often seen in certain southern Florida cities. By now bridge fishermen along the Miami River in downtown Miami are quite blasé about the great creatures that quietly materialize from the depths and disappear again. As a matter of fact, manatees grazed on the bottom of the river before the city was built.

There's often a method behind this seeming preference for civilization. When a winter cold snap chills the air, the warm-blooded manatee has no defense. As the water cools, it seeks the warmest spot available. This may lead it upstream to the tepid outflow from a power plant or to join others at the upwelling of a constant-temperature spring. Sometimes several huddle together in shallow water to share body heat. If none of these measures works, the manatees die. Recent unseasonably cold winters have claimed many.

New World Indians hunted the manatee for food. To early settlers in the Americas, the meat resembled pork or veal. They saved the oily fat for cooking and for their lamps. They cured the hide and carved the bones into ornaments. Today, Florida law levies a five hundred dollar fine on anyone killing a manatee. Commercial hunting of Florida's crocodiles has helped protect the manatee population, but a modern menace—the speedboat—occasionally gashes one of the startled creatures.

Naturalists hope they're holding their own. It's hard to say. They're too shy, too difficult to count. One biologist, cruising through good manatee territory in Everglades National Park, reported one manatee every seventy-five miles. Until we know how to count them, we cannot even guess their numbers.

The three manatee species have one smaller cousin, the rare dugong, which lives along the shores of the Red Sea, Indian Ocean, and tropical western Pacific. Like the manatee, it often goes by the unromantic name of "sea cow."

Scientists aren't usually given to daydreams. But when it came to naming the sea cow group, they remembered the story of sirens whose beautiful songs lured sailors to their death and came up with the perfect scientific name.

You'll find it in any zoology book: *Sirenia,* meaning "the seductive ladies of the sea."

Bullheads

As I RECALL, it was a long, long day. There we were, cooped up in the schoolroom, and our fish were drying to a frazzle out on the lawn at home. We'd laid them there in their burlap bag late the night before when we returned from fishing. I never thought of them again until the middle of algebra class.

There was nothing we could do about them until we got out of school that afternoon. In the meantime they'd slowly toast in the sun. Hardly the way to treat a mess of bullheads, John White and I agreed as we met and commiserated in the corridor.

This shows how little we knew about bullheads. If they'd been trout or perch or some similar bits of finny frailty, we'd have had to donate the whole outfit to the rubbish pail when we got home. But the bullhead—or, if you prefer, mudcat, horned pout, or bullpout—is made of sterner stuff. Nine of our eleven fish were still very much alive when we arrived home at three-thirty.

John and I dumped them into a tub of water. Luckily, trees above had shaded them from the direct sun and the burlap had been damp enough to keep their skins moist. So all they needed to do was gulp a few times, deliver a few bubbles of appreciation from those capacious mouths, and wobble to get the kinks out of their stiffened bodies.

Then they went on swimming as if being yanked out of

the water at night and deposited in a clammy sack on some boy's lawn was something that happened all the time.

We studied the whiskered, muddy-brown creatures for a few minutes. Then we put them, tub and all, in our old pickup truck. Retracing our path to the pond, we solemnly dumped them back into the water. They'd earned their freedom, we figured, and we were glad to let them have it.

Many bullheads are nowhere near that lucky. True, there are a few fainthearted fishermen who'd as soon cut the line as try to extract a hook from that froggy mouth. After all, it borders on sleight of hand to wrap your fingers around a slippery bullhead without becoming impaled on one of the three defensive spines—one dorsal and one at each side—it erects in protest. And the grunting as it forces air in and out of its swim bladder doesn't make the job any easier, either. Still, as nearly anybody who's sampled the tender white meat of the bullhead will tell you, it's worth the effort.

But it's not in the frying pan that the bullpout is at its best. Follow it through the world of pond lilies and muddy bottoms and you'll find a creature of constant surprises. Everything about it seems calculated to help it survive in its dusky world with as much ease as a child skipping along a sidewalk. Old Whiskerface, even though he is seldom more than a foot long, is a veritable Christmas tree of adaptations. He may look funny, but he's built for business.

Begin anywhere. Start, if you wish, with those eight long, delicate barbels, or feelers. Two stick up in the region of the nostrils, two droop from the edges of the lips like a skinny walrus mustache, and four project downward beneath the chin. Feather-soft, they sag helplessly when the fish is out of water. In their proper element, each one is a marvelously sensitive antenna.

Loaded with taste buds and touch cells, the whiskers provide the fish with a running inventory of a thousand tastes, touches, smells. Some of the taste buds run along from the whiskers onto the chin and belly, too, so the bullhead can

131

often "taste" with its skin. I've seen a bullhead settle down with its tail gently resting on a baited hook and then turn and unerringly gobble up the worm.

It's an education to see one of these fish slowly cruising along just above the bottom, whisker-ends gently caressing the mud, and then watch as he suddenly nuzzles into the mire and comes up with a hidden worm or snail. Other times, he'll merely investigate for a moment, then go on. Having taste buds on the outside must be an advantage. The catfish can taste something before he eats it.

Work backwards from the barbels and you'll find more surprises. In spite of its looks, that generous maw has teeth which are little more than sandpaper. But with an anything-goes appetite and with most of its food half-buried in the mud, there's hardly a need for teeth. The bullhead just mumbles its way through the debris, picks up what is edible, and discards the rest.

In such a muddy world, keen vision isn't of much value, either. So, like the teeth, the eyes are just barely useful enough to get along. Small and weak, they're hopelessly nearsighted, but they can tell the difference between light and dark. Many a fisherman has discovered this when he suddenly loomed up on the bank against the sky and was treated to the spectacle of a bullhead making tracks for the deeper water away from shore.

Since a myopic mudpout oblivious to anything but gleaning a meal is a conspicuous target for a passing pike or bear, there has to be something to tip the scales in its favor. That "something" is the trio of murderous spikes, bane of the fisherman. Found on the leading edge of the top fin and of the two forward pectoral fins, each spike can inflict a nasty wound. Although it's not poisonous, the wound is compounded by the slime which covers the fish's scaleless body. When we were "stuck," we'd rub the wound with some of the belly slime; this seemed to help.

Normally the spikes lie inert, moving easily with every

slight graceful motion of the fins. Let danger threaten, however, and a set of muscles pulls each spike erect and rotates it into a special bony socket. Locked there, the spike can be depressed only by breaking it—a prospect that can spell the doom of any giant pike foolish enough to swallow such a living pitchfork.

The bullhead carries still another protective device: its coloration. A silvery fish would be conspicuous against the dark bottom. However, the brown bullhead, *Ictalurus nebulosus*—literally, "the shady catfish"—lives up to its scientific name. Varying from gray to brown with a subdued mottled pattern, it looks like an old stick as it lies motionless under a sunken log. Even its belly is dusky-colored. Its two close cousins, the less common black bullhead and the yellow bullhead, are sometimes found in the same pond. Differences between them are barely more than technical. They're all big-headed and spike-finned, with a ridiculous extra little adipose fin just in front of a squared tail (black-and-brown bullheads) or slightly rounded tail (yellow bullheads).

The bullhead has one thing more in its favor. A farmer and I witnessed this one hot summer when the farmer's shallow pasture pond had evaporated to liquid mud. The dried carcasses of several perch and sunfish lay on the bank. As we stood by the edge and contemplated the scene, a sudden motion caught our eye.

"Well, I'll be—" my friend said, as we drew closer. "Look at all the bullheads moving around in the mud. What do you suppose keeps them alive?"

The answer, of course, was the same one I'd discovered years before: If its skin is kept moist, the bullhead can soak up oxygen for hours—even days, if conditions are right. It gulps air into its swim bladder, too, in a sort of primitive breathing. In Africa, people sometimes wrap living catfish in wet moss, take them to market and store them, still alive, on the shelves until they're sold.

True catfish, by the way, are first cousins of the bullhead.

Or to put it more correctly, a bullhead is really a medium-sized catfish. There are about a thousand species of "cats" in the world. They range, on our North American continent, from tiny poison-spined "madtoms" of some eastern streams (apparently not in northern New England) to the blue catfish that may reach one hundred fifty pounds, in the Mississippi Valley. In between are some thirty species, including those occasionally brought up out of Lake Champlain. These may reach twenty pounds and are apparently the channel cat of the Great Lakes and southern waters.

Worldwide, there are saltwater catfish and the armored cats of tropical aquaria. Then there's the pugnacious electric catfish of Africa with its hundred-volt punch and the *wels* of Europe, which may top six hundred pounds. So it's quite a family.

Bullpout family life is just as interesting as the bullpout family tree. The bullpout enjoys a sheltered childhood, as fishes go. This begins with the making of a nest—often by both parents, sometimes by the father alone. Deserting the deeper water for the shallows near shore, the parents use mouth, fins, and tail to remove the silt until a pan-sized gravel area is uncovered. Then the female deposits a thousand or more eggs the size of B-B shot, which are soon fertilized by the sperm of the male.

Sometimes this is as far as the female goes in her matronly duties. She may nose off into the deeps, leaving her mate to guard the nest by himself. At other times the two of them are the very soul of parental watchfulness. They fan the eggs constantly and attack any fish or fishhook that happens to come near.

The brood hatches out in a week or two, depending on the temperature, and the babies soon turn into jet-black replicas of their parents. Now begins a baby-sitting marathon. Guarded often only by the male, sometimes by both parents, the youngsters swim off in a mass, looking much like an inky pancake. Hovering, circling slowly, or directing its line

134

of movement, the parent mothers the finny brood most of the summer. Sometimes the young are shepherded into the shallows where insect food is thick. Other times they're guided into a patch of sunlight, apparently only for a sunbath.

Finally, after several hundred mouths have gobbled down several million worms, snails, aquatic insects, and bits of plant and animal life, the little fellows are about two inches long. Now the pancake begins to fall apart. By autumn, each youngster is off to cruise his own bit of pond bottom. With the coming of winter he half-buries himself in the mud or merely finds himself a sheltered spot. There he stays until spring, scarcely moving.

When warmer days arrive, he stirs himself. Then, almost as soon as the ice has melted, he finds his forays enhanced by a veritable jungle of fishhooks festooned with such dainties as balls of dough, fillets of anchovies, chunks of overripe cheese, chicken livers, pieces of hot dog, pickled salmon eggs, and, of course, worms.

From then until the ice comes again, the fish that looks like an angler's nightmare, but tastes, as one old book says, "as good as the brook troute in the spring, with a grateful lack of little bones," has a constant struggle to keep out of the frying pan. It doesn't seem to matter much to the anglers, either, that the best "bullheadin' " is done at night; they'll still seek him out, even after dark. In fact, the bullhead is probably the first fish ever caught by many neophyte anglers, with the possible exception of the bluegill sunfish, another eager eater.

Old Whiskers, of course, takes it in stride. In the forty million years during which he and his ancestors have vacuum-cleaned their way through the mud of North America, they have probably faced lots worse than chicken liver and worms.

Besides, the bullpout's popularity was never higher than it is right now. After all, his range once covered merely south-eastern Canada and most of the eastern United States to the

Mississippi Valley. But enthusiastic settlers have long since toted him west. Often they'd fatten him up in a rain barrel until sometimes he'd hit a groggy weight of about three pounds and a length of twenty inches. Finally his public has stocked him in almost every state of the union. Now they've even hauled him clear out to Hawaii and Japan.

Such a happy state of affairs ought to bring a smile to any pout. Even if, admittedly, there *is* a string attached.

The Killer Whale

"THEY LEAP clear out of the water and come down smack on the other whale's back with a thud that makes your boat shake. And after they beat the other whale out of its wits, they force its mouth open, then tear its tongue to shreds."

Thus an old whaling captain recalled the primal conflict of the ocean giants—the attack of a school of killer whales on their huge, placid cousin whales. Twenty to thirty feet of black-and-white muscular terror when full grown, the killer whale is the undisputed monarch of the sea.

Behind the deadly drive of the killer's massive body lurks an equally massive appetite, justifying the panic which it causes in other creatures. There is one record of thirteen porpoises and fourteen seals taken from the stomach of a killer whale. No one who has ever seen a killer whale can forget the menacing rhythmic rolling of the whale's body in the sea, or the tall, scimitar-shaped dorsal fin slicing through the waves. In polar regions, seals dash madly onto shore and into Eskimo villages to escape these gigantic dolphins.

That's what a killer whale is, technically—a dolphin. Tourists on ocean liners often place bets on the friendly bottle-nosed porpoises or other dolphin species as they outrace the ship. But even the porpoise in its speed and grace is no match for the diabolical 25-to-30-mile-an-hour rush of its big relative. In fact, the porpoise is a favorite item on the killer's menu.

Like its smaller cousins—and, indeed, like all whales—the killer is a mammal. It needs fresh air to live. Baby killers, born with only the numbing cold of the salt sea for a cradle, are nosed to the surface by the mother for that important first gulp of oxygen. No one has ever witnessed the birth of a killer whale, but anatomical studies show that only one baby is produced at a time. Its gestation period is about one year and its life expectancy is another thirty or forty years after that.

The newborn whale is about half as long as its parent and starts life weighing at least three hundred pounds. Its first meal consists of milk supplied beneath the flanks of its fearsome mother. Since the killer whales travel in packs, the childhood of this seven-foot infant is a continuous round of activity as it follows the parent at full speed from one massacre to another. It is hard to imagine a young manhood more free from the attack of enemies. For no creature of the sea will challenge the killer whale.

Most of the seas of the world know the massive thrust of the tail-flukes of the "Terrible Orca," as the ancients called the killer whale. The black head with the white eyepatch rises above the water, followed by the great fin which, on the male, is as tall as a man. A quick gasp of air, and the apparition disappears with hardly a ripple. Perfectly streamlined, it races under water at full speed, then surfaces again one hundred yards nearer its victim.

Nothing that swims is safe from this rush, unless it be the sperm whale of *Moby Dick* fame. Even these are sometimes brought in by whaling ships with great gashes showing the attacks of killers.

The whale's greatest enemy is his own huge size. A stranded whale is doomed because the weight of its great body makes breathing impossible. Oddly enough, with the entire ocean to roam in, the killer whale, in its frenzy to capture a seal or walrus, sometimes follows its intended victim onto the beach where it lies marooned, its tiny eyes following helplessly every move of its prey. Unless saved by an incoming tide, the giant quickly dies, a victim of its own greed.

Captain Robert Scott, in the journal of his last polar expedition, tells of two dogs tethered on an ice floe that were spotted by a band of seven killers. The marauders swam around the floe, sizing up the situation, poking their heads far out of the water. Then they dived beneath the surface.

The next instant the whole ice floe heaved upward and shattered into fragments. The whales had come hurtling up from the depths and burst through thirty inches of ice to get at the dogs. Luckily, the splits in the ice were between the dogs and the tethers held, so neither dog was spilled into the water. The whales looked around for their prey and, with victory almost at hand, unaccountably gave up the game and vanished as silently as they had come.

They have been known to chase a baby walrus until it clambered upon the back of its mother in terror. Seeing this, the killer sinks from view, to come hurtling up beneath the walrus, hitting her with a paralyzing jolt which spills her baby violently away.

Although the killer may be found in many parts of both the Atlantic and Pacific, his taste for northern seals and southern penguins often takes him to polar regions. The Eskimos have a great respect for the "wolf that lives in the sea." They have long believed that these animals are actually packs of Arctic wolves that can take to a marine life at will.

Despite a lack of external ears, the hearing of the killer is well tuned to sounds in its watery world. Studies with dolphins indicate that they can hear high-pitched sounds and send them out as well. Underwater listening devices have picked out all manner of noises from a school of whales—clicks like a telegraph, squeaks like a rusty hinge. Echoes from these sounds may help them navigate in the darkness of night or in the gloom beneath an iceberg in a fashion similar to the sonar used by the Navy.

As an aid to its tremendous appetite, the killer whale has a large enough throat to enable it to catch large fish, sea birds, and even some seals and porpoises in its ring of some forty-odd pointed teeth—each one far longer than the fangs of a tiger—toss them into the air, and gulp them down whole.

There are few animals in the sea or on the land that show evidence of any greater natural intelligence. Some experts guess that whales may be among the most intelligent beasts alive, perhaps ranking with the dog and the horse. Some captive specimens of dolphins have been hard to train because of this very trait; they seemed to be trying to outguess their human captors.

The sperm whale runs thirty feet longer than the killer but it is peaceful and even playful when undisturbed. The blue-fish is just as greedy and some sharks are just as vicious. But for sheer size combined with devastating power and cunning, no living sea creature can compare with the grinning, puffing, black-and-white torpedo—the wolf that lives in the sea.

AMPHIBIANS AND REPTILES

Old Bloody Nouns

WE FIRST met him when Jimmy tossed his line into the water. Neither of us had seen that bullfrog sitting like a chunk of moss on the water-soaked log. But he saw the splash of Jimmy's cork and launched himself on it like a missile.

My startled brother gave the line a jerk but the frog had already swallowed the bobber. Now he began to poke the line into his mouth with both stubby forefeet. Every time he opened for another gulp the sinker pulled out what he'd gained. So he headed for the mud.

Jimmy let him have plenty of line to see what he'd do. As soon as the frog got into the mud the buoyancy of the cork floated him out again. So he kicked his way to the top and skittered all over the surface.

This time Jimmy tried to reel him in but the frog did a crash dive. In a moment the line went slack.

"Doggone. Got away," muttered Jimmy, as the cork bobbed to the surface. When the frog had had enough he just urped up the dinner that wouldn't stay down.

He created a commotion that must have scared every fish, so we hauled anchor. Then we drifted down to a new spot where things weren't so active. But hardly had we settled down before the bullfrog had the last word.

"Be drowned," he intoned in a triumphant bass over the water. "Be drowned. Be drowned."

My father used to say that it sounded like "jug-o-rum." My mother thought he was saying "knee deep." According to an old natural history book on my shelves, the early settlers used to call him "Bloody Nouns." That's what he sounded like to them.

It's hard to describe his sonorous, strangely pleasant call, but easy to do a rough imitation. Face into an empty kettle or pail. This will give a resonance to your tone. Reach the note of low C-sharp if you can. Then say, like a voice from the grave, "Bloody nouns. Bloody nouns."

If you try this near his lily pads, the old-timer himself may answer you. In fact, he's got so much musical talent that he'll sometimes chime right in with almost anything you say, if you say it in a low, quiet voice.

A few days after the attack on Jimmy's fishing cork, we took a friend to see him. Most of the earlier frogs had left the pond and only a single spring peeper still called on that June evening. The sleepy trill of the toads had nearly spent itself, too, although we could hear a few from across the pond. But the bullfrog cared not at all that he was alone. "Be drowned," he suggested, as we quietly poled the old boat toward his log.

When we got there he was nowhere to be seen. But his basso profundo continued, seemingly right in our ears. Carefully we scanned the lily pads out of which the end of the log projected.

" 'Spose he's in on the shore?" Ralph asked, tilting his head to analyze the sound.

"Nope," said Jimmy. "Shore's too far away. That log must be hollow, and he's sitting inside it."

The log was hollow but there was no frog. Jimmy scratched his head. "He's not here and he's not over there on the shore. Then where in heck is he?"

The thought hit us all at once. We leaned over so quickly that the boat almost upset. Jimmy was the first to discover him. "There! Down on that log about a foot. And say, he's got a friend."

Sure enough, there were two frogs. Although the bullfrog is by nature a solitary creature, our friend had sung his solo well. Kicking in long, powerful strokes, a lady frog must have sped her way to his log a short time before. Now he clasped his arms about her middle, there beneath the surface. Oblivious to our peering faces above, he groaned his underwater serenade right in her ear.

With every declaration of frog-love, a resonance-pouch beneath his throat swelled like a double chin.

"But how can he sing under water?" asked Jimmy. Experimentally, he held his nose and made a grunting sound. "By gosh, it *can* be done!"

The waning day put an end to our prying into their private affairs. But the next morning three curious boys were back in the ancient boat. Old Bloody Nouns was silent but we poled toward his lily pads anyway.

A film of scum floated near his log. I went to skim it away so we could see better. It resisted my hand so that I looked at it more closely. The "scum" was hundreds and thousands of black eggs the diameter of a pencil lead. Each one was surrounded by a tiny sphere of clarity in that gelatinous mass. The whole affair was nearly two feet in diameter.

Sometime during the night, the two frogs had surfaced. Aided and encouraged by the viselike grip on her abdomen, the female had released her masses of closely packed eggs. The male, possibly triggered by her movement or by the decreasing diameter of her body, had released his sperm also. The fate of their section of frogdom rested on the chance that the two products would drift together safely in the still water, thus fertilizing the eggs.

We put a few dozen eggs in an old bucket. Then Jimmy shaded his eyes and looked down into the water. "Do you suppose we could find either of the parent frogs?"

He poked with the long pole at a muddy object on the bottom. At once it burst to life and kicked out for freedom. It dashed into the muck at one place after another so fast that we couldn't follow it. Then all was quiet, save for four or five muddy clouds in the water.

The bullfrog was in one of them, waiting for the silt to drift down on his back in a perfect camouflage. The transparent "third eyelid" over his eyes would enable him to watch what was going on from his hiding place. His skin would soak up enough oxygen from the water to keep him supplied for an hour so we pointed the boat toward home.

"Think they'll mind because we're taking a few of their eggs to hatch?" asked Ralph, as we carried the sloshing bucket homeward.

"Of course not," said Jimmy, who had looked up frogs in our nature book after we'd met Nouns the first time. "They don't take any care of their eggs at all. Once they've laid them, they forget all about them. The female deserts her mate and her eggs, too."

When we got home we put the eggs in a bowl of water. We could see the dark upper side of each sphere and the lighter lower portion. The lighter contained the yolk that was to nourish the embryo through hatching. In a day the eggs took on a football shape. Then in a few more days they began to look like stubby, dark little eels. They turned back and forth in their transparent prisons. Finally they made their way out, about a week after we'd gathered them.

"I wonder what they eat," said Jimmy. We had put a few old leaves and sticks in their bowl and a film of algae had begun to form on everything. "Suppose they'll find enough to eat in the gunk at the bottom of the bowl?"

His question was answered a day or so later. After the yolk was gone from each fat little belly, the pollywogs started in on the debris like miniature vacuum cleaners. Their mouths rasped and scraped and sluiced up the scrapings. We could see the tiny coiled intestines, like delicate watch springs, change color beneath the transparent skin as they became loaded with green algae. Two of the pollywogs had died and their siblings took them in stride, nibbling them to pieces, cleaning them up without a trace.

It became apparent that we weren't set up to feed 'wogs, so we took them back to the pond. As we released them, we were astonished at the appearance of the other eggs. They were just beginning to hatch. The pond water was cooler than the bowl on our sunny windowsill and the tempo of life had not been nearly so fast.

This dependence on the water temperature has a tremendous significance. For amphibians are forever at the mercy of the climate. They have to take their living conditions as handed out by nature while we warm-blooded mammals take our own weather with us in our veins.

Thus old Bloody Nouns may remain a pollywog for two and a half years in Nova Scotia, his larval period prolonged by long winters and short summers. At the other end of his range, he may go from egg to adult in a year in Louisiana.

Here in this Connecticut pond we saw pollywogs which stretched four and five inches from their scraper lips to the tip of the vertically finned tail. They had hatched out probably two years before. In spite of their advanced age, they showed little resemblance to their father. Tiny hind legs dangling uselessly from the end of their abdomens marked them as frogs, but the undersized eyes and the small puckermouths were more like those of fish.

Jimmy's book told us that this fishlike stage condenses in a few months what scientists believe happened some three hundred million years ago. At that time, an amphibianlike fish crawled up on some early mudbank and thus became the first land-dwelling vertebrate. From this humble beginning developed the true amphibia, and eventually the reptiles, birds, and mammals. So, in a way, as we raised our frog eggs, we were looking backwards through a telescope past cavemen, sabre-tooths, and dinosaurs, back to that momentous time when feet replaced fins and lungs supplanted gills. Our pollywogs, turning into frogs by absorbing their finny tails and poking out new arms and legs while they developed air-breathing lungs, were in a way repeating that pageant before our eyes.

Surveying all this from his log sat old Nouns like a goggle-eyed grandpa. Occasionally one of his offspring would drift to the water's edge at his feet. Then he'd look at it with paternal interest. Or at least so we thought until one day a fine three-incher popped up for a breath of air.

Nouns had seen him coming. Just as the 'wog hit the surface, so did the frog. Before our astonished eyes, he crawled back on his log, with just the tip of a tail protruding from his mouth.

"Wow!" said Jimmy. "No wonder there have to be so many bullfrog babies. Even their own parents are lined up against them!"

We loved to feed him. He would jump at anything that moved. Once I managed to stretch my hand toward him and wiggle the fingers. He attacked them in a flying leap. As he clamped down I could feel the row of tiny teeth in his upper jaw. They were like sandpaper.

"The book says they'll snap at a fluttering leaf," Jimmy suggested helpfully as I surveyed my skinned knuckles. "Even at ducklings and little turtles, too. One got into a water hazard on a golf course on Long Island. He killed himself eating too many golf balls."

The air above the pond was alive with insects. If a dragon fly or beetle happened too close, Nouns blitzed it without effort. His jaw would snap open, the sticky tongue would flick out, and the insect seemed to jump into his mouth of its own accord. Then, as he swallowed, he'd blink those huge eyes solemnly into his head. As they bulged down into the roof of his mouth, they helped the food along.

"I wonder if he eats bees," said Jimmy, looking at a honeybee on a water lily blossom. So, to experiment, we knocked a bee into the water and then let it crawl up on the log. But Nouns would have none of it. He wouldn't touch a hover fly, either, a harmless insect that closely resembles a bee. Our frog didn't jump at *everything* that moved. Somehow his vision could pick and choose and his impulses could check themselves.

We tried to guess how large he really was. We finally managed to lay a yardstick beside him. He was nearly six inches from nose-tip to the stub where his pollywog tail had once been. The day we'd seen him with his lady, she had appeared even larger. Our books said the record was about eight inches, with a weight of about one and a quarter pounds.

He was good at color changes. In the sunshine he'd be a bright spring green. On dark days, when it was cold or when he tried to hide in the mud, he'd turn almost black. Color cells in his skin would expand or contract, thus making him darker or lighter. His cream-white underside was probably good camouflage against an enemy gazing skyward from below.

The only time we ever saw Nouns in danger was when a snapping turtle drifted by as he was floating on the surface. So stealthily did the turtle approach that we thought it was just a chunk of debris. But Nouns saw his enemy just in time. He did a quick surface dive a split-second ahead of the turtle. As he dove for the bottom, he let out a stream of bubbles. The turtle, just behind him, snapped and bit at the bubbles. In so doing, of course, he missed the frog.

We tried to imitate a snake by dragging a rope in front of him. He puffed up his body and ducked his head. Thus he presented an unswallowable object in defense against this manila serpent.

The pollywogs, however, were not so fortunate. Tragedy stalked them everywhere. We saw some of them in the ice-tong grip of giant water bugs whose pointed beaks sucked their body fluids. Other predatory insects waited at every turn: water scorpions with their hooked arms spread wide, diving beetles, water boatmen, water tigers. Fish and snakes helped complete the nightmare that winnows down some ten thousand pollywogs in a patch of eggs to a few hundred froglings two or three years later. Even then the struggle goes on. Herons and mink and raccoons have their own stomachs to fill.

A friend of mine made me aware of still another danger faced by the bullfrog. We were drifting along in the old boat near the hundred square feet of pond surface that our frog called his own. "Want to see something?" I asked, as my eyes picked out Nouns sitting on his log.

We drifted closer. Suddenly Irv sat bolt upright. "Look, Ron!" he cried. "Look at the size of the frog on that log! Boy, what a nice meal of legs *he'll* make!"

Shocked, I explained that Nouns was sort of a special friend. "We've never even caught him in a net, Irv. Besides," I said, "he trusts us."

Irv took my explanation in good grace but I doubt that he fully agreed with it. He told me he'd rather have a fricassee than a friendly frog anytime.

Now that the thought of frog legs had been brought up, we were more careful about showing him to people. Still, one day I got to wondering just how chunky he really was, so I caught him. Immediately he screamed. His cry was like that of a child—high, shattering, open-mouthed. I quickly let him go and never violated our pact again.

One time as we floated up to his log, we could see that he was tangled in something. It seemed to cover most of his body. He was busily engaged in getting rid of it. Then as we looked closer, we understood. He was shedding his skin. As he peeled it off, he poked it into his mouth with both hands. He looked as if he was swallowing his own winter underwear.

Bullfrogs, we discovered, have been spread to many parts of the world. They live eight or ten years in captivity but are difficult to raise because they must be fed moving prey.

Although this insistence on moving food is a bane to frog-raisers, it's being studied today by scientists. A frog can pick out a single living insect in a whole tray full of dead ones. Scientists hope that they can find the secret of an eye that apparently sees only what it wants to see. Then, perhaps they can adapt it to camera use in underwater photography or weather satellites.

Our boyhood interest in Nouns, however, was uncomplicated by thoughts of satellites. We enjoyed him merely for being the sober old creature that he was. And the pond was strangely empty when the owner of the muffled croak dove into the October mud for his six months' nap.

Perhaps he sleeps there still. There was no welcoming bellow to greet us the next summer. But his tadpoles were there and I don't doubt that one finally took his place on the log. We sort of lost interest after our friend was gone. Possibly even now he grumbles in some watery heaven where the air is full of dragon flies and there are no snakes, snapping turtles—or small boys.

Friendly as a Beartrap

WHEN HE isn't disrupting traffic somewhere, he's supposed to be busy cutting down the duck population. Or if he's not doing that, he'll get blamed for spoiling somebody's fishing. And if you believe the tales about him, the snapping turtle spends half his remaining time (1) biting broom handles in two, (2) living longer than rich Aunt Minnie, and (3) building up an impressive avoirdupois of nearly one hundred pounds.

All these tales contain at least a grain of truth. More than one motorist has swerved to escape a wandering snapper in the road. And I recall a regular "turtle jam" on the Massachusetts Turnpike when one of the huge determined reptiles stood its ground in the middle of the highway to the delight of camera-carrying tourists.

To find out how the snapper affects the hunting and fishing, however, you've got to pry into its private life. And since the critter is about as friendly as a beartrap, there's very little prying that can be done. After all, those sharp horny jaws can give you a nasty cut. So it's safer just to guess at what it eats.

Actually, the facts are as interesting as the fancy. Any animal that can trace its family tree back to the days of the dinosaurs is bound to pick up a few quirks along the way.

Perhaps the best way to inquire into the life story of *Chelydra serpentina*, "the serpentine water monster," is to begin where most of us first meet it. This is when we find the wanderer along the road. Nearly always such a turtle is a female. Sometime during May or June, in the New England latitudes, the urge comes upon her to lay her eggs. So she hauls herself out of her pond or deep stream-bed. Then she goes in search of a suitable place.

During her pilgrimage, the female wants nothing to do with anybody. If she's disturbed, she strikes out with open mouth. She doesn't pull in her head and legs as most turtles do. Sometimes she lunges so hard that the effort carries her off her feet. And if she really gets warmed up, she'll wade into battle and actually chase you. Of course, you can get away—but it's an eerie feeling just the same.

Probably the snapper's temperament is to compensate for what it lacks by way of a shell. Although the upper shell is hard and sturdy, with strong sawtoothed edges at the rear, the lower shell is little heavier than a piece of cross-shaped leather. It couldn't begin to cover her soft parts, which stick out in a dowager's bulge on all sides. So, apparently, the snapper goes through life on the premise that the best defense is a good offense.

A female may find just the spot of earth to hollow out for her nest only ten feet from the water's edge. Or she may travel half a mile. She walks with a gait that's positively prehistoric —shell raised well off the ground, stumpy webbed feet digging their strong claws slightly into the earth at every step, huge head thrust forward, intent on finding the place for her eggs.

But beneath that sturdy shell beats a truly feminine heart. For the snapping turtle may investigate or ignore apparently good, diggable earth for hundreds of feet—and then stop at a spot that's just like dozens she's rejected.

She digs a quart-sized hole, or larger, in the sand or loam with her hind feet. Hunching over the hole, she lays some two or three dozen round, leathery eggs. They're about half the size of golf balls. Scooping the soil back in place, she pats and scratches it until the evidence of her work is hidden. Then she walks away without once having looked at her nest. This is the full extent of her maternal duties.

The eggs lie in the summer soil, developing with the warmth of the sun. Although they were hidden well by the mother, they're sniffed out by skunks, raccoons, and bears. Indians used to prize the eggs as delicacies, too.

A normal summer will bring the babies out by September. At the limit of their range in cool southern Canada, the eggs may remain through the winter and hatch the following year. Florida and Texas, the snapper's southern range, may produce two broods yearly, while Montana turtles, near the northwestern limit, produce but one.

A baby snapping turtle is born with all the delightful personality traits of his parents. Put your finger near his head and chances are he'll strike at it, even if some of the eggshell is still clinging to him and he hasn't absorbed his yolk yet.

How does a little turtle half a mile from water find his way to the pond? "Actually," an aquatic biologist told me, "many times he doesn't. Crows, grackles, hawks, small mammals all consider a baby snapper fair game, even if he's just a few minutes old. The little fellows run a regular gauntlet after they're hatched. But the turtles that survive seem to head in the direction of the largest patch of open sky, which usually leads them to a pond or stream."

Once arrived at the pond, the tiny turtlet with his half-dollar-size shell sinks into watery oblivion, emerging now and then as the fearsome creature about which all the tall stories are told. In the process of growing up he spends his next few years sampling nearly everything that moves, from snails to worms to tadpoles. Snappers may eat plenty of plant material, too. We examined the stomach contents of about twenty of them in a zoology course. Some were a third full of water weeds.

One time I watched a snapping turtle stalk a frog which was half-buried in the mud. The turtle moved forward almost imperceptibly. When it was near enough, it opened its jaws and closed them with a snap. The sudden inrush of water sucked the frog into its mouth.

Another time my father saw a snapper walking slowly over the bottom of a stream. "I could see it from where I was standing on the bridge," he recalled, "so I tossed a pebble at it. When it settled to the bottom the pebble made a little puff of mud. Right away the turtle jabbed at the mud. So I threw some more pebbles. It jabbed at every one."

What about the duck hunter's claim that the snapper pulls baby ducklings under the surface and eats them? Or how about the wail of the fisherman that the snappers are catching all the fish before *he* can?

"There's undoubtedly truth on both counts," my biologist friend told me when I asked him about ducks and fish. "Snappers will take ducklings when they get the chance. But so will big bass and pike. And the snapper eats these fish, too.

"Look at it this way," he concluded. "The snapper is part of the natural scene. He's as American as they come. If he's such a menace, how come the early settlers found ducks enough to blacken the sky and fish in every lagoon with nobody around to save these critters from the snapping turtle?"

At any rate, little snappers grow into big ones, aided and abetted by various unwilling victims. Just *how* big a snapper may get has been the subject of many a hot-stove argument at country stores for generations. Seldom does a large snapping turtle shrink in size when people repeat stories about him. But sixty-pound individuals *do* exist. And a snapper with a fourteen-inch shell *can* carry a man around on his back. Of course, considering the turtle's amazing reach and speed of strike, the man had better not be barefooted.

The age of the oldest snapper can't be weighed on the scale or counted like growth rings on a tree. And since the irascible fellow makes less than a charming captive, there are few family records to go by, in the manner of a pet parrot or goldfish. Even under the sheltered conditions of a zoo, few snappers have been kept alive more than twenty years.

As to the broom handle diet, it's hard to say what one of the outsized seventy-pounders would be able to do to a chunk of wood. A twenty-pounder in my possession was just about able to chomp a pencil in two. And a pencil is far from a broom handle.

There's still another theory about snapping turtles that needs a closer look: that they're always of such a mean disposition. One day a high-school lad brought me a medium-sized snapper of perhaps ten pounds. "Where'd you get him?" I asked.

"Oh, I saw him dig down in the mud," was the easy reply, "so I waded in and felt around 'til I found him."

Apparently the boy wasn't just lucky, either. The snapper is in its element under water and seems to be far less on the defensive. But I'll leave that method of capture to someone else. There's always the chance that the turtle doesn't know he's *supposed* to be gentle and harmless in such situations.

Of course there are other times when the snapping turtle forgets himself. After a long winter spent in the mud or in the interior of a muskrat house that he has casually taken over, the snapper emerges in spring with an eye for romance.

Snapping turtle courtship is about as tender as you might suspect. The male nuzzles the female, nipping at her head and feet, and banging her shell with his own. Sometimes in shallow water both sexes have been seen cheek to cheek, gulping in water and forcing it out again in a gurgly love song. Although the eyes of these creatures are good, the males at this time seem to suffer from myopia—or perhaps merely overenthusiasm—for one male has been known to cuddle up to another before its mistake was made clear by the surprised party.

Mating turtles take little notice of what's going on around them. Often it's at this point that the old New England farmer would capture one and put it in a big barrel half full of water. He'd feed it table scraps all summer until it was fat and prime. Then, when he slaughtered it, he'd have several pounds of the finest, tenderest white-and-dark meat that ever graced the table of a gourmet at fancy prices.

I've eaten snapping turtle a number of times and I don't blame the farmer and his barrel one bit. Nor do I wonder at the indignation of the epicures in Baltimore who heard that their beloved entree was to be placed under a bounty like a common criminal.

For even if he isn't the largest, the oldest, the fiercest creature that lives, he's certainly one of the tastiest that ever bit a broomstick in half—almost.

Those Spring Peepers

EVERY MOTORIST who has driven along the open highways of the East on a balmy night in April knows the sudden high-pitched crescendo of sound that betokens a swamp along the roadside. Even passengers on a speeding train may hear the shrill chorus of myriad pipings above the roar of the wheels.

Ask the traveler what causes the sound and he will likely shrug his shoulders. "Birds," he may say, or "Some kind of insect."

Unless he knows the true nature of this little songster, he will probably never consider that it might be a frog. But frog it is—one of America's smallest amphibians; indeed, one of the world's tiniest vertebrate animals—the diminutive spring peeper.

Few Americans have seen this little creature, even in jars of preservative in a museum; fewer still have seen it alive. Yet its song is as emblematic of spring as the call of the first robin or the shy nod of the first violet.

If you were to look right at him in his native habitat, chances are that you would never see him at all. Ranging from a deep chestnut brown to a light tan, he clings tightly to a reed or twig, alert and motionless, blending perfectly with his surroundings.

Once we see him, however, we note that he has a pronounced "X," or cross, on his back, running diagonally from left shoulder to right hip and from right shoulder to left hip.

This has led scientists to give him the name of *Hyla crucifer* —the crossbearer.

Turn this little frog over and his whitish underparts give him away at once. This coloration protects him from underwater predators as he floats on the surface.

Even if they were able to see him, he might pass undisturbed, for his tininess is unbelievable; he could sit comfortably on your thumbnail. The weight of such a small body is unnoticed by any but the most delicate scales. It may take from ten to fifteen of them to weigh an ounce.

This little frog is anything but small in voice. In the throat region is a thin air sac which communicates with the mouth cavity through tiny openings. When he is about to sing, the throat sac becomes enlarged like a translucent bubble, serving as a small but effective resonance chamber.

The high-pitched sound produced is so penetrating that this midget can be heard for half a mile. Thus, if our voices were in the same proportion to our size as the tiny Spring Peeper's, a man weighing one hundred sixty pounds could be heard twelve thousand eight hundred miles away.

As soon as the frozen grip of winter begins to relax, these restless little songsters come out of hibernation, seeking open spots where the sun is warmest and where there may be a small spring pond. They hop along the forest floor and the meadowland, guided by a sure sense which draws them toward water. Often they may sing as they go, but the real chorus does not begin until they are in the swamp.

One by one they slip into the water, which is sometimes so cold that small pieces of ice may still be floating in it. Undaunted by the frigid temperature, they climb onto a bit of leaf or grass and launch into the shrill, intermittent song which continues for the next two months.

At first the sound from the swamp is hesitant and broken. The few first-comers sing somewhat timidly, as if conscious of their tiny size. But day by day new frogs arrive to take up the chorus, and the songs become steadier and lustier. As the days pass, the chorus becomes one constant torrent of high, shrill sound, pouring out of the swamp with such volume that the individual songs are lost.

It seems as if nothing could still the song of the peepers. In fact, if we were to shout ourselves hoarse, it would have little effect. But let the shadow of a hawk streak across the pond and the chorus is stopped instantly. Or let a muskrat crawl up on the bank where half a dozen songsters are piping, and they will immediately flatten themselves against their perches, silent and watchful.

However the exuberant song will not long be quiet. Life runs too strongly in these diminutive creatures to be denied expression for more than a few minutes. Soon one more venturesome than the rest emits a querulous call, as if to inquire whether all is well. Almost instantly, two or three others answer from nearby, and their call is taken up by still others until the swamp is once again a riot of sound.

Why does the spring peeper, in common with most toads and frogs, go through this strange migration to the swamps and back to dry land? The immediate answer is, of course, so that the eggs may be produced and fertilized. But the underlying drive behind it hearkens back to bygone eons.

Careful reading of the fossil history of the rocks indicates that the first vertebrates to make the epic change from life in the water to existence on land were creatures which had many of the characteristics of our present-day amphibians. Regarded by scientists as primitive fishlike forms, they roamed the steaming forests and were able to exist in the thin, inhospitable, changeable veil of air, rather than the enveloping, cushioning water.

They grew more and more specialized as time passed, but were never able to break completely the tie which bound them to an existence in the water. The parents were compelled to return to lay their eggs in the water and the young passed their early existence there.

Today our spring peeper, millionth son of a millionth son

of these primitive forms, still follows the same blind urge. Spurred by the hospitable rays of early spring sunshine, he hurries to the swamps to fulfill his mission.

For the rest of the summer and fall, the peeper wanders about in the cool woods or the brushland near a swamp, catching the insects and other small creatures which are its diet. Although its tiny gold-flecked eyes apparently see quite well, they can distinguish only moving prey, and so it eats only living insects.

Peculiar sticky discs on the ends of the toes enable it to climb up the surfaces of objects, and it may be seen many feet above the ground. If we touch one of these little fellows on his branch, he merely clings closer to the bark; if we disturb him too much, he will unhesitatingly launch himself out into the air, landing on the ground unhurt.

Like all other frogs, the *Hyla* is unable to maintain a constant body heat and goes into hibernation with the onset of winter. Warm days may call him forth for a few brief hours during a January thaw, but he soon goes back to his slumbers, out of reach of the killing frost.

But when the ice melts from the ponds and the buds of the pussy willows show gray, he begins to stir and soon his exultant piping is again heard in the swamps, and we know that the earth has made a full swing through its orbit and spring has arrived at last.

INSECTS
AND SPIDERS

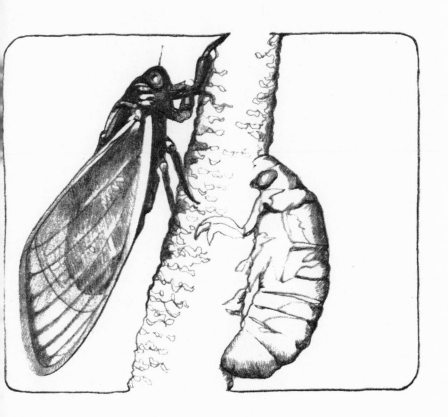

La Cucaracha

THE COCKROACH shared its shelter with the first caveman a million years ago. Long before that it saw the last dinosaurs disappear. Indeed, the cockroach had been around some fifty million years before there were *any* dinosaurs. This puts it in a position to celebrate its two hundred fifty millionth birthday right about now.

It also stamps the cockroach as one of the most successful creatures of all time. Any modern housewife who has had to deal with one can tell you that. So could the ancient Egyptians, who had to resort to trained cats to keep its numbers in check.

But just *how* successful the cockroach has been and by what means are only now coming to the attention of scientists. In fact, so impressive are its qualifications that the lowly cockroach is now being used for studies in genetics, space travel, and cancer.

Consider the matter of cave dwelling, for instance. With a vast span of existence on earth behind it, the cockroach had already weathered about every peril of life. So when those first ape men moved into the cockroach's caverns and discovered fire and invented the wheel, the roach just moved over and let them discover and invent. This may in fact have been just what it needed for a new lease on life. For fire and wheels provide warmth and mobility—two top requisites in the roach world.

How did this "Model T" among insects get such a running start in life? Certainly there's nothing striking about its looks. The flattened, brown body of most cockroaches is only moderate in size, as insects go. Those modest, straight wings carry it only on modest little jaunts—and any entomologist will tell you the power of flight is a great advantage to an insect. Some roaches are even wingless.

And the cockroach's "collar," or forepart of the thorax, spreads forward so the roach must forever carry its head so the chin rests on the chest. This no doubt gives it a marvelous view of little else but the earth beneath its nose.

But the cockroach cares not for these disadvantages. Indeed, through the trial and error of millions of generations, it has managed to turn them to its favor. The cockroach's body is smooth and polished and about as easy for an enemy to grasp as a slippery watermelon seed. The roach's small size and flatness allow it to slip into all kinds of cracks and crannies. It can even telescope its abdominal segments, or extend them, if necessary, for a better fit.

Its lack of air power has forced the roach into a ground game. It has astonishing running ability. A large roach in good condition can scoot fifty yards in a minute on a pavement. That's half the length of a football field. In China there are even cockroach races with championships, betting, and selective breeding for good, fast stock.

The running is not all of the straight-line variety, either. A roach can feint and dodge like a hockey player. It can even run upside down. Once, while camping, I tried to overturn an old log near a path. A piece came off in my hand, scattering a family of wood roaches over the hard earth. In a moment they had scuttled to safety, all but one, which took longer. Having had the misfortune to fall upside down, it valiantly rowed itself along anyway. Its frantic legs knocked against juts of earth and debris and propelled it in the direction the rest of the roaches had taken.

Another safety device is the roach's "collar," which protects its vulnerable neck. Since the head is flexed well beneath it, the collar acts almost as a knight's helmet. Concerning the myopic view the roach must have of life, all that really seems to matter is the difference between light and dark. And this a roach can tell, somehow, even when its great compound eyes are painted over by inquisitive scientists.

Protruding from the cockroach's body at several points are some of the keenest sense organs imaginable. Those threadlike antennae, usually longer than the body, waft daintily forward. They caress the ground lightly or hang in mid-air. Their delicate hairs pick up the smell of potential food and sample the character of the pathway ahead.

The cockroach antennae even serve as sightless periscopes. When I was stationed at an air base in the tropics, half the knotholes of a certain wall of the mess hall were occupied by a pair of long antennae each. They poked out into the room, waving gently, smelling and feeling the air, and disappearing if we came too close.

Outside the roach's mouth are small, fingerlike objects, the palps, and they're studded with taste hairs. These compound the problem for purveyors of roach poison, for they enable the roach to taste food before it eats.

Additional hairs on the body, wings, and legs make a roach literally a bundle of nerves. Actually, most insects have these body hairs but the roach goes them one better. At the tip of its abdomen are two extensions, the cerci. In addition to "tasting" the air, the cerci have another surprising function. They're sensitive to vibrations, low sounds, and wind currents. So even when a cockroach is engrossed in feeding, its tail radar is in operation to quickly detect the stealthy approach of an enemy.

All this gadgetry has enabled the roach to make itself at home almost anywhere. It's been found in skyscrapers and submarines, streamliners and stratoliners. To judge its success as a traveler, merely look at the names it has collected.

Entomologists call it *Blattella germanica,* the German cock-roach. Germans call it the Russian roach. The Russians think it's south European. New Yorkers called it the Croton bug in the belief that it had come from the Croton aqueduct. The American cockroach probably came from Africa on slave ships. The eastern roach is found in the West, and so on.

Life begins for a cockroach almost anytime that conditions are favorable. With *Blattella germanica* this is often, but not always, in spring. How spring can be detected in the hot, moist world of steam pipes and sculleries is some-what of a question, but probably such identification is related to the decreasing period of darkness for these noc-turnal creatures as they explore the building. Many of the two thousand two hundred fifty cockroach species, however, don't worry about the coming of spring. They just mate when convenient.

Following mating, the female may produce eggs within a period of two weeks or more. She extrudes them into a small capsule which she carries around attached to her abdomen.

Depending on the species, the roach may finally deposit the capsule in a sheltered nook, covering it with debris for concealment, or may retain it in her body. Here the young will develop, burst their cases, and emerge at a run. This gives rise to the improbable spectacle of a mother giving birth to thirty-tuplets.

Little roaches, or nymphs, resemble their parents in most ways but size and wing development. *Blattella germanica* nymphs are scarcely larger than grains of sugar but they're complete with tiny antennae, tail cerci, and all. They stay in the same general area as the mother. Thus the burgeoning family resembles a hen with a brood of lively chicks. There may be a crop of older brothers and sisters, produced a month before, to complete the clan.

Juvenile roaches grow, as do all insects, in spurts. Each phase is punctuated by the shedding of the skin. The new skin is pliable and elastic. The nymph takes in air to expand itself as much as possible before the skin hardens, then proceeds to fill itself to the bursting point again. After the last molt the wings expand from buds on the thorax, and there's your new adult.

The whole cycle, egg to adult, may take only three months. But even while they're nymphs, the youngsters seem to travel under some special form of blessing. Not only are they speedy and tiny, but if some enemy catches them, they merely shrug it off—literally. Captured by one of its legs, a young roach twists until the leg breaks. After escaping, it casually proceeds to grow a new leg.

There is one more big factor to the cockroach's success—its appetite. A roach can eat almost anything—it's about as fastidious as a garbage disposal unit. It may consume its own shed skin or carefully remove the glue from a sheet of postage stamps.

Since the cockroach is a seasoned traveler, it has been known to nibble the nails of sleeping sailors on ships. It also indulges in more prosaic fare, such as table crumbs, the dregs of bottles, and forest litter. A salivary juice it spreads on its food to soften it before eating gives the characteristic musky, roachy odor.

Oddly, though, the roach is one of the cleanest creatures known. A cockroach may lick and preen itself more than a cat. "Sodium fluoride roach poison wouldn't work half so well if its victim wasn't so neat," an entomologist told me. "After walking through the powdery chemical, the roach licks it off its feet and legs. Then it ends up with one whopping case of indigestion."

But some of these very factors in the roach's life have caused scientists to look at it with new respect. More prolific than rabbits, the roach is a natural for genetics studies. Scientists can obtain three or four generations a year with no more outlay than a few loaves of bread, some apples, and a handful of dog food. And the indifference with which a roach parts with its body members seems to indicate it is insensitive to pain.

In the course of laboratory studies, scientists have learned still more about these astounding creatures.

The cockroach is perfect for long-distance space tests. Not only can it withstand more than one hundred times the radiation dose which is lethal to man, but it is almost totally indifferent to "G" forces, those shattering gravity stresses which cause man to black out in high-speed turns. Aloft in a space capsule, it would need next to nothing in the way of food, drink, or air. In fact, a roach can survive for hours with all of the tiny breathing pores along its body sealed tightly with paraffin.

The cockroach may be useful in still another way. For as man beats the sunlight in its journey around the Earth, he is becoming concerned about biological clocks, those little-understood timing devices which regulate our many body processes, including hunger, sleep, fatigue. Here, too, man may depend on the cockroach.

One question is: Just where is the "clock" located? Apparently, at least in the roach, it's in a gland near the brain.

A roach can be kept at room temperature but its "clock" can be stopped for a few hours by pinpoint refrigeration. Then, when the insect is returned to normal, the clock takes over, causing the insect to live in the past, as it were.

A "clock" gland can also be transferred to a second roach which is minus its own gland, and the replacement "clock" will take charge on its own schedule.

In the course of these studies, scientists stumbled on an unexpected puzzle. They discovered that if normal glands were transplanted into roaches after a twelve-hour time lapse, the host insects developed intestinal cancer and died. So now the doughty insect may be called into battle against one of man's most dread diseases.

The cockroach has been enlisted in another battle, too— against itself. Captive roaches are being used to discover ways of controlling their wild relatives. U.S. Department of Agriculture investigators have isolated a sex attractant from females that brings the males at a dead scurry. Then poison bait or traps do the enamored suitors in.

Another method of control is to treat males with powerful shots of radiation until they are sterile. Then they are foisted on the unsuspecting roach population. The hope is that these supercharged males will mate with wild females, and that the females will then lay worthless eggs, or none at all.

So, even as we force one of the earth's oldest inhabitants to help us with our twentieth-century problems, we hunt new ways to prompt its demise. Things look bad for the cockroach. Pretty soon it might be as dead as a dinosaur.

But don't count on it. After all, with its long and illustrious history, it's hardly what you'd call a fly-by-night.

My Shoe-Button Lady

THREE FEET from my typewriter the eyes of one of the world's most dreaded creatures are fixed on me. She takes her leisure on a silken couch, watching, waiting. Scarcely an eighth of an inch of fragile glass separates me from her fangs.

She is tiny for such a venomous creature. A school boy's marble is heavier and larger. Yet, drop for drop, the fluid which oozes from special organs into her hollow fangs is far more deadly than that of a rattlesnake.

She has lived on my desk for nearly two years. All this time she has been in a carefully sealed glass house that is never opened except to introduce food and drink. She has lived twice as long as some two hundred of her brothers and sisters. Yet at this moment she appears to be just in her prime.

My shoe-button lady? One of nature's most fascinating creatures, whose rounded black abdomen resembles the buttons on old-fashioned shoes—*Latrodectus mactans*, the black widow spider.

Her silken couch? The web she spins to trap her victims—one of the most perfectly formed strands known. Her sealed glass house is a mayonnaise jar, upside down, with the cap screwed tight.

She came to me along with several score of her brothers and sisters two years ago, the gift of one of my biology students. At this stage she was a tiny pearly egg, encased with the others in a sturdy bag of silk that had hung in the web of her mother. A few days after I received it, the bag opened at one end and the spiderlings began to crawl about. Nearly invisible at first, they were a transparent orange-tan and white.

It was soon evident that I could not satisfy their appetites. Although I dropped countless aphids and other tiny insects into the web, the spiders had no scruples; if an aphid was not handy when hunger overtook them, they captured a brother or sister.

After a week of this, my family was down to less than half its original number. The survivors had increased greatly in size and their appetites kept apace. I had to work mightily to keep them supplied. Every time I forgot for a few hours, there would be fewer mouths to feed.

I tried separating them into individual jars. In this way I saved ten females and a dozen males. By now they were each about as big as a grain of rice and handsomely dressed in red, orange, and brown. The little males had begun to take on the adult appearance—long-legged, with slender bodies. The females were more robust. They spun nondescript little webs up in the corner of their jars where they waited for their ration of two insects a day.

The black widow, like other spiders, insects, and crabs, grows by shedding its outer covering. Unlike a bird or mammal, which has an inner framework of bone to build upon, the spiders and other arthropods have their skeletons on the outside. To grow, the swelling body bursts its confining prison, pulls out of its walls, and forms a new covering which hardens quickly. My spiders shed their skins half a dozen times, changing size and color each time.

The males kept the juvenile pattern, decked out in colored bands on the legs, with stripes and dots on the abdomen. The females lost their gay colors and assumed the appearance of their mother—a shiny, beady black. On the underside of each was a deep red or orange-yellow hourglass figure, some-times with the central portion missing.

I fed my charges daily. The only air they needed they re-ceived when I opened the jar to put in a fresh insect. Some-times I'd give them a drink of water on the end of a tooth-pick.

It took about three months for them to mature. By this time the females were about twice as large as the males. I introduced two of the males into the jar of one of the largest females in the hopes of getting a sack of eggs. But the black lady had no such romantic thoughts in mind. Swiftly, with a loop of viscid silk drawn from her abdomen, she entan-gled the two young hopefuls and proceeded to dine on them.

How was I going to mate these spiders if they treated each other this way? Then I remembered something from a book on spiders. It said that the black widow will not eat her mate if she is well fed. So my next attempt at playing Cupid began by stuffing two lovely ladies with all the food they could eat. After several days, when they showed no further interest in the flies which buzzed around in the jar with them, I came along with my bridegrooms.

Transferred to a larger jar where escape was possible in case his lady love should have a change of heart, one of the males took courage. Cautiously he wooed his deadly para-mour, twitching the strands of the web in a special fashion to assure her that this was no ordinary fly.

The bride-to-be showed little apparent interest. To an am-bitious male spider, this is a sure sign of impending success. Presently I noticed that his suit had found favor, for she twitched the web right back. Before long he had made his way to her side. His partner, stuffed with food, could find time for romance.

The mating was a strange process. Male spiders place the sperm on a bit of web, then store it in the knobbed tips of the palps, their leglike feelers. There is no direct genital contact. My enamored male spun his intended in a delicate silken shroud, then placed the contents of the palps in her reproductive opening, which is up near the chest region. Following this, she easily broke free of the flimsy bonds of affection he had thrown about her.

After mating, what would happen to the male? Would he be eaten by his partner, who would thus fulfill her name of "black widow"? Some of my books said his doom would be sure; many of them, however, disagreed.

Apparently the female was still satiated. She showed no further interest in him. He stayed with her in the same web for several days, until one morning I found him dead. She hadn't attacked him, for he was not entangled or bound in any way. He had died a peaceful death.

His mate became sleeker and rounder. I named her "Lady" with tongue in cheek, recalling her treatment of earlier mates. About six weeks after mating, she spun a closely woven brown silk bag in her web, nearly half an inch in diameter. The next month a hundred new spiderlings emerged, giving me another round of inhabitants for my improvised glass houses.

Lady eats one insect a day. To catch it, she goes after it with a lasso. Drawing out some fresh silk from the spinnerets of her abdomen, she holds it between her two hind legs. Backing swiftly toward the victim, she deftly flips it through the air in hope of snaring a meal. Again and again she may make this backward toss with the sticky silk.

Finally she makes contact. Her efforts rewarded, she draws out more silk in a rush, turning her victim end over end until it is securely trussed. All this may take less time than to tell about it. A darting, bobbing black widow in pursuit of her prey is a marvel in motion, especially when you consider that this is all done in reverse on a shaky web and solely by the sense of feel.

A few minutes ago I gave Lady her daily food. Her poison, so dreaded by mankind, seems to be just as effective on insects. Although the victim was a moth twice her size, the numbing venom took hold speedily. Within five minutes all activity had ceased.

Spiders, by the way, have a special method of feeding. Not only do they suck the body fluids of their victims, but they eject special juices into them by means of the hollow fangs. These act on the tissues, rendering them semiliquid and capable of being drawn into the spider's body. A fly which has been thoroughly worked over by a spider may thus be little more than a mass of indigestible legs and wings.

Black widow venom is indeed a fearful substance. It seems to have an almost immediate effect on the nerves, muscles, heart, and digestive system. Characterized by extreme general pain and often by severe intestinal cramps and abdominal rigidity, black widow bite has been diagnosed as appendicitis, renal colic, or food poisoning. More than one person has been operated on for acute appendicitis following an unnoticed black widow bite.

Although fatalities on record are few (chances are twenty-five to one you'll recover if bitten), the pain is such that the victim wishes he *would* die. The traditional "snake bite cure" with tourniquet and suction seems to be of little value here. Your best bet is to capture the spider for later positive identification and rush to the doctor. He may give you an injection of antivenin to counteract the poison. Calcium gluconate put into the bloodstream also brings amazing relief from the agony of muscular cramps.

If she's such a bad actress, why is Lady allowed a place of honor on my desk? There are many reasons I could put forth, which only another naturalist would understand. At any rate, the main ones, which apply equally to your chances with her species, are these:

Lady, like any other black widow, is shy and inoffensive. She puts her trust in flight, rather than fight. If I take her out of her jar and place her on the table, she loses no time in finding shelter. If I disturb her web, she retires to a far section of it or drops meekly to the floor. If she were still guarding an egg-sack, she'd be lots more dangerous, just as a hummingbird has been known to attack an eagle near its nest. Or if she were hungry, she might give my tweezers an experimental nip when I remove the corpses of her past meals.

Suppose, however, she escaped from her half-pint jar? Suppose she mated and produced more egg-sacks, which she was prepared to defend with her life?

There is, of course, this possibility. But such a chance already exists, for the black widow has been reported from every state in the union, even including my adopted Green Mountain State of Vermont. And given free choice, Lady would rather have an old lumber pile or abandoned foundation in which to build her nest. She'd probably waste little time in leaving forever my brightly lit, typewriter-clacking office.

Oddly enough, this desire for seclusion has resulted in an appreciable number of bites. A favorite habitat of the black widow is the outdoor privy, especially the underside of the seat. If you have such a privy still in existence at your farm or summer camp, it should be screened and well lighted and hinges should be attached to the seat so that the underside can be inspected periodically. Although the biting powers of this half-inch creature are definitely limited, the tender skin of this area of your body is readily penetrated by her fangs. A large percentage of spider bites have taken place in outdoor privies.

With such a virulent poison and the willingness to use it under certain circumstances, why are there so few recorded deaths from the black widow (fifty-five in thirteen hundred known cases)? It's because of the limited amount of poison which she can inject in one bite. Her whole body is scarcely larger than a good-sized kernel of corn, so the total amount of venom she has available cannot compare with that of a six-foot rattlesnake. In addition, she may have just paralyzed some insect and have little poison left when forced to bite a human.

Despite their lethal weapon, the black widows have effective enemies which help keep their numbers in check. Besides their own tendency toward cannibalism, they have to reckon with the attacks of spider-hunting wasps. These insects deal a paralyzing sting and then store the spider as food for their young. The spider hovers between life and death for weeks in a state approaching suspended animation.

Other predators, such as lizards, certain birds, and some mammals, dine on the black widow when they have the chance.

The most effective natural check, perhaps, is a tiny insect which flies into the presence of death to deliver its telling blow. A small fly with the impossible name of *Pseudogaurax signata,* it threads its way between the strands of the web until it comes to rest on the egg-case. Here it lays a series of gleaming white eggs. In less than a week, the tiny larvae push their way through the fibers of the sack until they are inside. Here they feed on the eggs of their fearsome host. In about a month from the time their bold little mother visited the web, they fly away as full-grown adults, leaving the black widow guarding an empty shell.

With her eight legs and eight eyes, her habit of hanging upside down in the web, her lethal poison, and her attitude of watchful expectancy, the black widow is not the most charming of insects. But chances are that she will be around for a long time. For my shoe-button lady and her relatives have been found in nearly every country on earth.

Insects of Vermont

IT'S SURPRISING what effect those tiny creatures with all the legs have on our lives. Consider a year in Vermont, which admittedly has its share of insects. You'll find they not only lend variety but even help to set the scene for the season.

Take a summer day, for instance. Many of the birds are silent. Their family duties are coming to a close and they are far less vocal than they were in spring. But the air is by no means still. For as August and September approach, so does the annual heyday of the insects.

Walk through a Vermont countryside and you'll see the creatures everywhere. The sunshine catches them as they wing through their few hours of adult life. Over the expanse of a meadow their multitudes give a shine to the air. The sound of their movement is only half-heard but it forms a background for the summer day.

A grasshopper crackles in flight as it springs ahead of your steps. A treetop cicada, looking like a huge fly, vibrates a drum beneath its abdomen with a ringing buzz. Hundreds of anthills erupt their winged queens and drones as if at a signal. These they send in misty swarms for their mating flight. While the leaves hang limp and the hay cures in the field, the little lives race headlong.

You can almost tell the temperature just by watching the insects. The hotter it is, the faster they go. Metallic blue or green tiger beetles run along a country road faster than you can walk on a hot day in the sun. When it's cooler, however, they have to use their wings to keep ahead of you. Dragonflies dart over a pond in their search for gnats and mosquitoes. When the sun is hot they can outmaneuver almost any bird. But let a cloudbank cool the air and they may slow down to where swallows and flycatchers can catch them. Then you may see one of nature's countless food chains—mosquito is caught by dragonfly which is caught by swallow.

You'll find these minuscule Vermonters everywhere. Last year I stopped by the road at Townshend Dam. The sandy soil looked sterile and bare. But soon I saw it was pockmarked with hundreds of little funnel-shaped pits as if there had been a tiny air raid. Each pit was about half an inch deep. If an ant blundered into the pit, a shower of sand grains would be thrown up from the bottom. These would come cascading on the ant, tumbling it downward to the waiting jaws of the pit's hidden occupant—the squat-bodied, six-legged little bulldog of the insect world, the ant lion.

In the bushes by the road I could see other insects. A horde of caterpillars had stripped the leaves from a cherry tree. These nibblers in turn were falling before the onslaught of large greenish-blue beetles with a reddish sheen. These were the fiery searchers, sworn enemies of caterpillars and helpful allies of man. The caterpillars were also under aerial attack as a number of flies darted down and laid eggs on their bodies. These eggs would hatch into larvae which would devour their unwilling hosts. Like the searcher and the dragonfly, these insect allies of man were doing what no insecticide could ever do—actively seeking out and killing its prey.

There were numbers of other little dramas enacted over that summer countryside. They take place everywhere and are not hard to find. All you need do is pause by the road or take a country walk.

A herd of Vermont's famous cattle, for instance, represents a bonanza for thousands of flies and other insects. If you look closely you'll see hornets and yellow jackets too. These relatives of the wasp, so unwelcome at a picnic, are now squarely on the side of the farmer. They dart at the flies, snatching them and carrying them back to feed to the young hornets in the nest. And the constant hum of the hornet's cousin, the bee, serves as orchestration for the summer afternoon.

The green of summer changes to the gold of autumn. Now a new dimension comes to the Vermont landscape. Until now, except for the sound of their movement in the vegetation, most insects have been silent. But as many insect youngsters change to adults, they find new voices. Tree crickets, grasshoppers, field crickets, katydids, even some ants and beetles add their sounds to a chorus which swells daily.

An autumn afternoon may be so filled with the noise of insects that no single voice can be recognized. Actually "voice" is not the word to use, for the chirp of a cricket is no more a voice than the snap of your fingers. Neither is the buzz of a locust nor the sizzle of a katydid, for that matter. All those autumn sounds are made by an assortment of legs scratching on legs, wings rubbing together, or one body part scraping on another. No insect has vocal cords, although a few ants make a grinding noise with their jaws if you disturb their nests.

Like the summer activity of insects, these fall sounds reflect the temperature. In fact, if you can learn to identify the monotonous, high-pitched musical note of the snowy tree cricket, you do not need a thermometer. All you need is a watch. Count the tree cricket chirps in fifteen seconds. Then add forty, and there, within a degree or two, is the temperature.

There may be even more insect voices than we realize. One autumn day I was watching a certain grasshopper as it rubbed its legs together. All I could hear was a faint whisper. But then my children, several feet away, pointed out that another grasshopper was rubbing its legs, too. It was in perfect rhythm with my own specimen. The sound was too faint, or perhaps too high-pitched, for our ears, but the 'hoppers had no trouble keeping together. Studies have shown that probably many of our other common insects also make sounds that are beyond human hearing.

When I taught biology, autumn was the time of year when students brought in the greatest number of insects. Seldom a day would pass without its praying mantis or butterfly. Seldom a day passed, either, but what some coccoon would quietly hatch out. Then it would announce its new status with a flutter of wings at the window while the students delightedly suspended all study to watch.

There's something frantic about all this insect life, though, at this time. Beetles, flies, grasshoppers pay little attention to the food around them. All season they've been stuffing themselves; now the time has come to insure the success of future generations. Thousands of them mate, lay eggs, and drop nervelessly to earth. Ants harvest the bodies of the fallen insects and dig their tunnels deeper in the soil. Woolly bear caterpillars hurry across a road, following some instinct to a hiding place beneath a log.

A few of Vermont's butterflies even go south for the winter. Some may go as far as Texas or Florida. Daily flights of monarch butterflies can be seen over Lake Champlain in autumn, following the valley. They may have other butterflies as companions. On one trip across the lake I counted more than sixty admiral butterflies, skippers, and swallowtails which flew over the ferryboat. The mourning cloak butterfly hibernates in hollow logs. Still other species are represented by wintering eggs, pupae, or caterpillars.

Finally one night the temperature plummets below freezing. Some of the insects fall to the grass roots where they are partially protected. But by morning the frost has killed thousands. The autumn chorus is ragged now. After two or three more freezes it fades away except for a few forlorn individuals that still scratch out their little call-notes in the warmth of a late October afternoon. Then at last they too fall silent.

Even in Vermont's celebrated winter, the insects are still with us. Of course, hundreds of species are represented only by eggs, but hundreds more are adults slumbering beneath the bark of trees, the clapboards of houses, or within hollow logs. Many of them are poised to take advantage of any break in the weather. I've seen mourning cloak butterflies flitting over the snowfields in a January thaw. One tiny insect, the snow flea, has a gray body which absorbs the heat of winter's sun. Thus it can walk around on top of a snowdrift. Sometimes it exists in such quantities that it colors the drift gray, like soot.

If you look along the banks of a Vermont stream on a mild winter day you may find an insect which seems to live its life backwards. When most other insects are stiff and unable to move, the winter stone fly makes its way from the stream. It crawls upward and creeps on top of the snow. Like the snow flea, it has a dark body and soaks up the sun's heat in a few seconds. Now it can run, mate, and even fly, improbable as it seems.

Some kinds of crane flies and caterpillars may suffer from insomnia, too, and creep over the snow as in a dream. Almost every warm day will bring a few cluster flies from an attic or a hollow tree, where they buzz at windows or take short flights in the sunshine. Ladybird beetles—among the few insects even a squeamish person will permit to walk on his hand—are called out by the warmth, too. In fact, so lightly do the winter insects slumber that one student in my college biology class made a collection of fifty species between New Year's and Easter vacation.

Some winter insects make their own shelters. My students often brought in a number of coccoons that they'd found wrapped in leaves or hanging from twigs. The eggs of the gypsy moth are placed on a little mattress and covered with a blanket made of the hairs from the mother's body. And the ball-like gall of the goldenrod fly is a familiar sight as it waves on a dead stalk in a winter gale. Open it up and you'll find a grub the size of a grain of rice. I'm told it's an excellent spring bait for trout.

Finally the optimism of the winter insects bears its fruit. The cold relaxes its grip and spring comes to Vermont. Of course, "spring" is a relative term in the Green Mountains. It's hard to say just when it begins. But on a March night you may see small brown moths flying in the glare of the auto headlights—"sap moths," my neighbors call them, for they appear at sugaring time. The mourning cloak appears again, this time for good. As the buds burst on the trees, so do countless numbers of insect eggs. They are triggered by the same returning sun which brings life to leaves and blossoms.

It brings life to ponds and streams, too. Down in the river below my house a number of people in odd clothing wander slowly along in search of trout. I join them whenever I can. Many of us use worms or other natural bait but there are a number of purists who use nothing but dry flies. These flies are often most successful when they imitate another of Vermont's insect populations—the myriads of stream dwellers that emerge from the water and fly around for a brief period of egg-laying. These are the mayflies, stone flies, caddis flies, and alder flies.

A Royal Coachman or Silver Doctor may look like a bunch of feathers at the end of a fishline but from beneath the surface it's supposed to resemble an insect which has fallen to the water. Thousands of fishermen annually stake their vacations on these feathery imposters.

Fortunately a Green Mountain spring is not blessed with an overabundance of some of the critters that make life miserable in other outdoor areas. Mosquitoes, black flies, and gnats have their day each year, it's true. However, the "day" for each species lasts only two weeks or so. By July they've peppered their last tourist or fisherman, laid their eggs, and disappeared.

The Vermont year has its colorful seasons, its leisurely ways, its constant call to the tourist. And beckoning in their own small way, with squeaky voices and fascinating habits, are the hosts of insects which help set the Green Mountain scene.

The Cicadas Are Here!

When certain worried homeowners and farmers in the eastern United States telephoned to agricultural extension services that June day, they found they had plenty of company. Calls had been flooding into the offices of state universities and county agents since May.

A Cape Cod, Massachusetts, resort owner was astonished at the windrows of large insects that littered the sand of his beach. Farmers in Pennsylvania and eastern Long Island wondered what to do about the "big, noisy bugs." New Jersey suburbanites, Kentucky mountaineers, Carolina tobacco farmers, and residents of half a dozen other eastern states sent out urgent pleas for aid.

In all these places you could hear the cry: "The cicadas are here!"

In certain places in each state the foliage had become covered with slow-moving insects larger than an inch in body length. Although they did not feed on trees and shrubbery, their vast numbers created a general alarm that rapidly spread over the countryside. Everywhere the molted skins of the insects could be seen clinging to trees and shrubs while their newly emerged inhabitants fluttered noisily in the upper branches.

The cause of all this commotion was the seventeen-year "locust," more correctly known as the periodical cicada. After spending a growing period of seventeen years underground, the cicadas were emerging from the cool dark earth. Maturing in different sections of the country in certain years, this was their year to emerge in parts of the East and Middle West.

The nymphs crawled stiff-leggedly up the side of the nearest tree or shrub, finally coming to rest a few feet above the surface of the ground. Within a few minutes the longitudinal split appeared in the back, and the crowding shoulders humped their way through. The head followed, then the legs, and the cicada pulled itself forward out of its old nymphal shell, which still clung to its support.

Forward and upward it crawled, waving the crumpled wings in the air, the body color turning from creamy white to brownish black. Minutes after the nymphal case had first split, the cicada had come to its full beauty: dark body with yellow legs, eyes the color of rubies, transparent wings two inches long and glistening with rainbow hues in the sunlight.

The opening scene had been played in one of the most poignant dramas that exists in nature. Everywhere—on the sides of buildings, telephone poles, picket fences, mailboxes, and especially the trunks of trees—there were dozens, hundreds, thousands of cicadas emerging. The cast-off nymphal skins clung like gigantic buds on the branches of trees and bushes.

Upward and still upward the insects toiled, as if they could not get enough of the warm sun after the long years of darkness. Up the main trunks they crawled, along the larger limbs to the twigs, and finally to the tips of the topmost leaves.

Here the second stage in the drama was enacted. Crows, jays, robins, blackbirds, sparrows, and scores of other insect-eating birds were noisily feasting and gorging themselves on this insect food suddenly concentrated within their reach. The ground became littered with cicada wings that lay like snowflakes beneath the trees, glistening and sparkling. Nature's great equalization process was in full sway, cutting down the millions of insects lest they overrun the earth. Although the cicadas feed hardly at all as adults, they spend their nymphal life underground drinking the sap from the tree roots, and thus nature has provided that the demand shall not exceed the supply. Even as the birds were devouring the cicadas, thousands more came to take their places, and the noisy struggle in the treetops continued day after day.

Then, almost beyond the power of the human ear to comprehend its exact beginning, the third stage in this drama began. Starting with a faint trill as of some small bird or frog, a new whisper of sound swept through the trees and was gone. In a minute it was back again—and died away a second time, a third, a fourth. Perhaps the fifth or sixth or twentieth or hundredth time it did not die away; it began to swell in volume until it became a steady, high-pitched hum. The amazing sound-drums on the backs of the males were beginning to vibrate and the tone resounded from one tree to another.

At night the sound ceased and the feeding birds flew off to bed, leaving the treetops as silent as they had been a week before. With the warm rays of the morning sun, however, the chorus began anew. Midday again quieted the clamor, but it began afresh toward evening. Thus the first week or two passed, while the ranks of the cicadas in the trees were continually augmented by the myriads still emerging from the ground below.

Finally, the heat of midday could no longer still the chorus. About two weeks after the first cicada had been reported, the steady sound swelled to gigantic, overwhelming proportions. It was everywhere, seeming to come from the ground, the trees, even from the skies, as male cicadas flew from one spot to another, singing as they went. The individual songs could not be picked out and the chorus went on with deafening insistence—the sound of life itself, lived to the fullest by creatures privileged to exist a few short weeks in the sun.

Such was the tremendous urge and drive behind the song that nothing short of death would still it. A cicada might be seized by a bird or house cat, or perhaps it might fall into a pool already littered with bodies of dozens of its fellows. No matter; the song would not be denied. It would continue until the songster no longer was alive.

The next scene opened when the singing was at its height and the air itself throbbed with sound. The males began to search out the females amidst this frenzy of noise and activity. No longer were individuals content to clamber over one another in an effort to get to the top of a bush or tree; they began to pair off for the great purpose which seems to motivate all life—the perpetuation of the species. In pairs they lined the branches and limbs, the males still singing, the females silent and alert. The mating process of the cicadas is wonderfully simple. A brief attachment of the bodies of the males to the females, and the process is over.

All the years of slow toil through the earth, the laborious crawling of a bursting body up into the sunlight, the emergence of a creature of many colors, and the terrible gauntlet through the ranks of the chattering birds—all have been in preparation for this brief moment in the sun. The principals in this drama have played their roles without rehearsal and without flaw, driven by some tremendous urge and led by some commanding law beyond our understanding.

The work of the males was done. One by one, their songs died and their slowly numbing legs lost the grasp on the limbs to which they had clung. Down they fluttered, perhaps catching briefly to a leaf or twig, but slowly, inexorably being drawn to the earth from which they came, until they lay amid the debris of the nymphal shells which they had split apart a few weeks before.

The task of the females was not yet finished. The needle-like ovipositor, normally half-hidden beneath the abdomen, lanced deep into the tender bark of the branch on which they rested. Egg after egg was deposited in the green tissue until the body of the female, which had been bursting with its precious cargo, became empty and shrunken. Then, like the males, their legs gradually lost their hold and they too fell to the ground. Now there were no adults left, only the eggs, like tiny grains of rice that appeared lifeless and hopelessly inadequate for the long task ahead.

A few days later the shells of the eggs began to crack and tiny nymphs struggled forth. Soon the limbs, trees, and shrubs were once again peopled, this time with tiny antlike replicas of the big nymphs that had struggled upward so recently.

With no guide to point the way, they followed the same plan which has been carried out for past ages, feeding for a few brief weeks on the life-giving sap of the upper branches, then dropping to the ground and burrowing down to the tree roots. Down beneath the surface into the cool soil they burrowed. There each attaches itself, its slender beak inserted into the tissues of the root which furnishes its only food for the next seventeen years. The sound and the clamor have died away. The earth is silent once more. Not one living periodical cicada can be found aboveground over the length and breadth of this area. The years will be long before it returns. Other broods in other years will appear in places but not for seventeen years will the first full-grown nymph of that brood make its way aboveground.

Sounds of September

THERE ARE new sounds in the air. Although the birds no longer proclaim their territory with song (for they have no nests to guard), the countryside is far from quiet.

Chief among these noisemakers are members of the most musical family on earth: crickets and grasshoppers. All summer they have quietly pursued their lives in the grass; now they burst into song. Field crickets call from their hiding place beneath small stones. Grasshoppers and green false katydids sway on their blades of meadow grass. In the trees, the true katydids say their names over and over in measured tones. As children, we used to lie in bed and listen to their "katy-did" or "she-did." We often thought of the old wives' tale that the song of the first katydid usually meant six weeks to frost.

There's a good reason for this sudden rush of song so late in the season. The insects couldn't have sung a note before if they'd wanted to. With the exception of a few grasshoppers that spend the winter as adults and a lucky cricket or two, most of the songsters start from an egg each spring. Newly hatched nymphs lack wings to crackle and buzz, or the proper gadgetry on their hind legs with which to fiddle a wispy tune. Nymphs must grow and shed their juvenile skin a number of times until they have wings and scratchy legs.

The sound of triumph comes first from one grass clump

and then another as each insect announces his new status. Cool days postpone the debut of many youngsters and slow the songs of the others, but each warm day swells their numbers.

So attuned are the insects to the conditions of weather that it's possible to tell the temperature by listening to a cricket's call. The best species for this is the snowy tree cricket, whose steady, musical, almost monotonous note can be heard from clumps of bushes and the trunks of trees. At a pitch about three octaves above middle C, its tempo is faster on a hot night, slower when it's cool. To judge the temperature, count the number of cricket chirps in fifteen seconds. Add forty—and there's the answer in degrees Fahrenheit.

Crickets and their relatives aren't the only voices to be heard. Cicadas in the trees drone out ringing notes. As with many insects, the males do the singing, vibrating a tympanum on the abdomen and magnifying the noise by a special "sound mirror." Down in the grass, an anthill disturbed by a passing animal may erupt with a faint piping noise, the gritting of the jaws of the workers as they rush to defend the nest.

All through autumn, the myriad sounds from earth will continue. A light frost will stop a few of the noisemakers but the rest will sing on. Finally, the killer freeze will arrive and they will all be silenced.

TREES AND
OTHER PLANTS

Plant Ballet

ONE DAY while I was hoeing a row of peas one of the vines came away from its wire support. Laying the vine back in place, I continued to work. When I returned an hour later, I found that the plant had already taken hold of the wire. Two tendrils had curled entirely around it; a third was well on its way. They had moved through a complete circle with just about the speed of the minute hand of a clock.

This motion is only one small facet of plant behavior. All kinds of plant movements go on constantly in every garden. Were our eyes able to sense it, we'd see the green world doing a fantastic, silent ballet.

Motion is a vital key to plant life. It takes place even in seed. Little appendages on some types of grass seed, for instance, are twisted like a corkscrew. Changes in humidity tighten or loosen the spiral. With each twist the seed is forced over the surface as it lies on the ground. Finally, it happens to lodge in a crack or crevice. Thus secured, its chances of success are enormously better than those of another seed that may be continually blown about.

Once a seed has found conditions right for germination, it must hold on to its location. First to appear in most sprouting seeds is the slender fingerlike root. Probing and seeking, the root quickly threads down through the grains of soil. Thus it anchors the seed in place. Radish roots may sprout more than an inch in twenty-four hours, putting out small branch roots as well.

At almost the same time, the plumule strives upward. Once above the soil it spreads its tiny leaves to take advantage of the sun. But the sun, of course, is not stationary. So many seedlings bend hour by hour, following the sun in its journey through the sky, keeping their leaves spread to the light. In the morning they point east; in the afternoon, west. Around them are thousands of other seedlings doing the same "dance." And over the surface of the earth, billions more follow the sun. Less choosy or less favorably located seedlings merely point at the brightest part of the sky and strive upward toward it.

As a plant gets older, its stem becomes thicker. Soon the entire plant can no longer move as a unit. But a reduced motion continues in the shoots and leaves as they spread themselves to the available light. They may rise and fall with dawn and dusk or change their angle of tilt so that the light strikes their surfaces as nearly broadside as possible.

Blossoms undergo a daily rhythm, too. Through the magic of time-lapse photography, the jasmine can be seen to open its blooms as the day fades, spreading its perfume for night-flying moths. At the other end of the cycle, the morning glory bursts shortly after dawn. Its nectar is for bees and other early fliers until the dew dries and crawling insects visit its blossoms.

Countless other flowers open and close as day comes and goes. A hollyhock blossom in my garden opens after sunrise, disclosing a bumblebee which slumbered, protected, where it had been caught in last evening's rain. And all around are thousands of other plants, struggling upward toward the sun, shouldering each other for that vital advantage that may mean success.

Perhaps the best-known example of homage to the sun is the motion of the sunflower. Hour by hour, the sunflower's huge disc faces the sun. In fact, so deeply ingrained is this daily pattern that a sunflower deprived of its light will continue its motion for several days, faithfully following the sun that it can no longer "see."

Light creates new arrangements in this "standing room only" world of plants. Pull a stalk of rhubarb from a clump; within a day or two all the other leaves have moved to fill the vacant space. The same thing happens when a weed is pulled from a lawn or, more slowly, when a forest giant falls to earth. Within a short time its neighbors shift to take advantage of the increased illumination and elbow room. And, of course, potted plants must be turned every few days for they too will lean toward the light.

Apparently, the ends of the roots and shoots guide much of this activity. Lacking eyes, the plant yet "senses" the sun through a few cells at its growing tip. Remove the tiny leaves at the end of the sunflower's stalk and it loses much of its ability to turn with the sun. Cut off the tip of a growing root and it may expand itself uselessly against a pebble instead of creeping around the edge.

Botanists have discovered growth substances in these plant parts which are responsible for much of this seeming sense of direction. Called "auxins," they stimulate the development of tissues and organs. Simply stated, the more auxin production, the faster a tissue will grow. When a structure is illuminated from one side, auxin production on the opposite (shaded) side is thus stimulated. Hence the structure is forced to bend as it grows.

A leaf, for instance, shifts itself to get the most light. Thus all of the leaves of a tree become arranged to take advantage of the illumination available. If an entire branch is completely shaded, whole leaves may grow to a huge size. Notice the next tree whose illumination varies from bright sun to heavy shade. The leaves in the sun may be less than half the size of those in semidarkness.

All around us is a green world of unseen motion. Leaves droop and curl under summer's heat, protecting the pores of their under surfaces from evaporation. My garden peas and other vines twist and climb, guided by auxins released on the stimulus of touch. Tomato and clover leaves become vertical at night, horizontal during the day. The oxalis folds its shamrock-shaped leaves at dusk, just at the time the evening primroses open.

Perhaps it's all summed up in a story from one of our Vermont town meetings. Two men had been arguing a proposal for some changes in the school system. Finally an old gentleman whose patience was nearing its end got to his feet.

"Why is it, Bill," he asked, "that some bean plants will twist around a pole to the right, while others will twist around a pole to the left?"

Bill didn't know.

"Do you know, Frank?" asked the old-timer.

"Why, no, I don't," said Frank, surprised.

"See," said the ancient Vermonter, "you're trying to talk about education. And yet you don't even know beans."

Which, with our tendency for taking our living world merely at face value, may say it for us, too.

Don't Count the
Spreading Chestnut Out

As WE neared the spot, I felt as if I were visiting a lost civilization. In my lifetime I had never seen a mature, healthy American chestnut tree. The devastating chestnut blight had seen to that.

Until now, all I had ever seen were a few sprouts or tragic, shiny-gray skeletons of once sturdy trees. Yet we were only three miles from living specimens. A single tree was as rare as a pearl—and we were about to see *eight* of them.

My parents had told me about the straight, durable wood of a chestnut. Fence posts made of it, they said, would last a lifetime; chestnuts had provided fences for thousands of farms before and after Abe Lincoln split rails.

Chestnut bark had tanned half the country's leather, they said. Its wood made planks, furniture, musical instruments. There were the joys of nutting, when the great crop of prickly burrs opened with the autumn frost. The nuts, the size of large grapes, were sweet with a taste all their own.

Then my parents soberly told me of the blight which had spread across America. As it passed, it laid waste to uncounted billions of board feet of America's single most important hardwood tree.

My friend, a forester, turned the car up the little country road. "So far," he said, "we haven't found a single blight-resistant American chestnut. When a tree gets the blight, it dies back to the ground. The next year it sends up sprouts from the roots. These sprouts grow until they're four or five inches in diameter. Then, suddenly, the fungus strikes through a crack in the bark. And you're back where you started."

That's what made these eight trees even more exciting: They seemingly should have been struck by the blight several years ago. Now they would be ten or eleven inches in diameter. This hardly compared with the hundred-foot giants of old, but they were not mere struggling saplings, either. They were young, maturing trees. In fact, when the forester had last seen them two years ago, they had produced a crop of buffy-brown nuts in their incredible prickly cradles.

Would they still be healthy? "That's what we're interested in learning," my friend said. "They're big enough now so that every growing season is an event. If they last much longer we think we've really got something."

But then, since Vermont was at the northern edge of the tree's natural range, there could be another factor. The disease might have fizzled out for lack of eligible prey before it got this far. So these eight trees might just be living on borrowed time.

My friend told me how another forester had quietly planted them fifteen years before. They had shown unusual promise, and his friend had wanted to get them growing well without fanfare. "If they don't show any disease cankers by this autumn we'll be able to experiment—" he began; he stopped in mid-sentence as we rounded a curve.

I stared at him. His face showed disbelief. "Well, see what they did to the road," he said softly. "There go our chestnuts."

He stopped the car, though there was little to see. The authorities had straightened and raised the roadbed. As so often happens, they hadn't concerned themselves with what was growing there. Those eight trees had fallen in the name of progress. The little chestnut grove was buried under twenty feet of gravel and sand.

This was just one small incident in the long, heartbreaking story of the last sixty years of the magnificent chestnut. Ever since the disease was noticed in the early 1900s, the tree has suffered, and often at the hands of the very people who love it best.

In fact, it was probably through an unhappy mistake that the blight reached here in the first place. Asiatic chestnut trees imported to this country were probably to blame. They had doubtless been exposed to this Oriental disease for centuries and had learned to live with it. The American tree, of course, had had no such opportunity to develop an immunity.

So close is the relationship between the species that the jump from one tree to the other was easy, once the conditions were right. The tragic part is that some nurseryman who loved both trees may well have been responsible for the fatal transfer.

No matter how it actually started, here was a field ready for the grim harvest. The village blacksmith's spreading chestnut; the sturdy woodland trees whose nuts fell after a frost with a noise like hail; the tall timber trees that represented thousands of miles of telephone poles and railroad ties—all were defenseless.

Progress of the disease was slow at first. Here and there a farmer puzzled over the loss of a pasture chestnut. Homeowners sadly surveyed the great swollen blisters that partially encircled the trunks of dying shade trees. In 1904 the disease came to official notice with the discovery of a few afflicted trees in the New York Botanical Garden.

Hardly had word of the new malady come to the attention of scientists than the blight reached menacing proportions. It fanned out from the New York City area. It struck into New England, New Jersey, Pennsylvania. Unhampered by any national quarantine law in those days, it traveled almost with a will of its own. It would affect all the trees in one area, then skip over hundreds of potential victims to strike in another town. Then, perversely, it back-tracked to make the devastation complete.

Worried agricultural experts tried to determine the means of its spread before it was too late. The disease was found to be caused by a fungus, eventually named *Endothia parasitica*. Like most fungal organisms, it reproduced by spores. These came from dry, blisterlike pustules on the bark. When a spore alighted in the smallest wound, it developed into a smothering mat of unseen threads. These threads invaded the vital tissues beneath the bark. Finally, they girdled the tree.

The most common means of spore dispersal is by wind. Dying trees were cut and burned in a dozen states to keep the disease in check. And in one sweeping gesture, a great mile-wide belt of healthy chestnut trees was felled in Pennsylvania. It was hoped the spread of spores would be halted. But the costly effort was in vain. The leapfrogging blight raced on, almost without pause.

Too late it was realized that there are two kinds of spores. The second type, embedded in a sticky matrix, oozed from dying wood like toothpaste from a tube. It readily clung to the feet and beaks of birds. Thus it could spread as easily against the wind as with it. This explained the spotty occurrence of the blight. And, in this case, it also brought to light another painful fact: The disease was probably carried on the axes and saws and clothing of the very people who were struggling to control it.

On and on went the blight. While the federal Plant Quarantine Act, belatedly passed in 1912, was a help, the damage had already gone too far. Infected nursery stock had been brought into areas to replace trees that had died. Spores on seeds lay in wait for years. Then they attacked the infant seedlings as they germinated. Utility poles and rough lumber with the bark still clinging also carried the disease.

Thus the unknowing introduction of the blight by man

was compounded by his unknowing spread of it. Birds, insects, and wind compounded it still further.

Preoccupied by World War I, America soon had little spare time for chestnut trees. And there were still some in fine health. "You will be happy to know," wrote a Connecticut mother to her doughboy son, "that the big tree on the lawn has escaped the terrible blight. So there should be plenty of chestnuts to stuff the turkey when you come home."

But her luck was probably shortlived. By the late 1920s the blight had blanketed New England. By the late 1930s it was groping toward Michigan, the western limit of the chestnut. By the late 1940s it had reached Mississippi and Georgia, the southern corners of the tree's natural range.

Now, at last, the spread of the disease slowed. There were no more chestnuts to conquer. The devastation was nearly complete.

Nearly, but not entirely.

And in that *nearly* lies a mountain of hope. When the last passenger pigeon died in Cincinnati on that September day in 1914, an entire species died with her. But the American chestnut is in a far better situation. Luckily, the blight has chosen to attack a tree with tremendous rebounding power. No sooner does it die than those sprouts appear, again and again. Sometimes they produce a crop of nuts even while the blight gnaws at their living tissues. Thus, in their faltering, they continually toss the torch to a new generation.

It is in those valiant little sprouts that hope for the chestnut still lies. One of them could produce a mutation making it resistant to the disease. Then too, there are still a very few large trees in the Midwest and in the southern Appalachians. They seem to have survived as if by a miracle, although their neighbors perished long ago. Perhaps one or more of these has become immune to the blight, like their Asiatic cousins.

A third source of hope lies, surprisingly, in those Asiatic

chestnuts—the very trees which brought the blight here in the first place. Perhaps some hybrid could combine the fine timber qualities and the delicious nuts of the American tree with the disease resistance of the more shrubby Asiatic species with their less tasty fruit.

At any rate, scores of individual scientists, foresters, and private citizens think it's worth a try. The battle, first begun so desperately sixty years ago, still continues. Instead of frantic measures like wholesale cutting and burning, such weapons as the grafting knife and the pollination brush are now employed. Reports of trees eight inches or more in diameter are carefully followed up. Every now and then there's a heartening breakthrough—like those eight roadside trees. Or, similarly, deep discouragement.

Headquarters for today's campaign are found in many parts of the United States east of the Mississippi. At the local level, county agricultural agents, county foresters, and state universities receive reports from campers, vacationists, and landowners who believe they have found healthy chestnut trees.

"We investigate every report if it seems promising," a county forester in Massachusetts told me. "A lot of the trees turn out to be beech or oak. After all, the three trees are closely related. In fact, it seems that the chestnut blight has adapted to oaks and stays hidden there, waiting for new chestnuts."

A chestnut spreads like an oak when it grows in the open. A number of oaks, such as the chestnut oak, have long leaves with rounded teeth on the edges. True chestnut leaves have sharp teeth—hence the scientific name *Castanea dentata*—and the leaves are eight to ten inches long. Beech leaves are similar in appearance, but smaller. In addition, beech bark is light gray and dull and smooth, while chestnut bark is shiny gray-green-brown, splitting into longitudinal ridges with age.

There's another tree that's often confused with the American chestnut, too: *Aesculus hippocastanum,* the horse chestnut. Together with the buckeye, its nuts resemble the European chestnut found in markets today. Horse chestnuts, however, are bitter and unfit for human use. And the true chestnut bears its leaves singly, while those of the horse chestnut are compound, like seven green fingers radiating from a central stalk. Horse chestnut flowers are showy, white-purple-yellow clusters in June, while the true chestnut displays erect, greenish-yellow catkins in July.

Weeding out the false alarms, some of the scientists have found a handful of promising trees. Many of these are near the limit of the old range of the chestnut: Michigan, Vermont, the southern Appalachians. Perhaps with few trees to spread it the disease just has a hard time sustaining itself. Perhaps there is some peculiar soil condition that is responsible.

Once a promising specimen is located, it may be investigated in several ways. Scions may be taken from it for grafting on hardy trees, such as the Chinese chestnut, at several sites throughout the country. The universities of Tennessee and Virginia, among others, have worked on this project. If a majority of such scions prove promising, this rules out special soil or environmental conditions that might have favored the parent tree.

The trouble with this method, of course, is that it is slow. Trees take years to mature. You cannot raise a generation in three weeks, like fruit flies in a laboratory. It doesn't even help to try to inoculate the juvenile scions with the blight. They have great resistance when young, but may die later. So it's a long, tedious process that may end in failure again and again. But always the hope is there.

A Vermont forester, the late George Turner of Burlington, was engaged in this work for many of his later years. He sent scions to a number of places. Among them was the Northeastern Forest Experiment Station in Upper Darby, Pennsylvania. Some of these grafts have "taken," and have produced fairly commendable trees. Others, dishearteningly, have grown for years and then died.

Another hope is in cross-pollination to produce hybrids. Here the pollen from one tree is dusted onto the flower of another in an effort to combine the good features of both or to fashion a new individual. Hybridization has produced the hard-working mule, disease-resistant wheat, giant-flowered plants, and heat-resistant cattle. Work on the chestnut has occupied some of the efforts of the Connecticut Agricultural Experiment Station at New Haven and the Northeastern Forest Experiment Station.

Russell B. Clapper and co-workers at Upper Darby produced a Chinese-American cross which shows surprising promise. The Clapper chestnut, as it is called, was planted in a plot in Illinois. There it reached a vigorous size of more than seven inches in width and a height of forty-five feet in seventeen years, fast for almost any tree.

"Some of the hybrid trees are very promising," says Richard A. Jaynes, associate geneticist at New Haven, "but their vegetative propagation is difficult. We have experimented with several propagation techniques and hope to find one that will be commercially acceptable."

In the meantime, there is still another point of attack. The American chestnut, whose demise began about the time the Wright brothers made their first flight, may receive help from another of man's discoveries—radioactivity.

When the seeds of a plant are irradiated, the genetic material in the chromosomes is affected. One sunflower I saw grown from irradiated seed had produced all rays and no disc—and hence no seeds. Treated rye seeds produced normal-appearing plants, but they had no chlorophyll. Irradiated chestnuts may just possibly come up with blight immunity. Plant specialists in Tennessee and Virginia, among other places, pursue this hope.

"We realize that our chances are not too great of producing a disease-resistant mutant," Dr. Ralph Singleton admitted to me, "but since there is a finite possibility of doing it we are going to irradiate as many seeds as possible." A former director of the University of Virginia's Blandy Experimental Farm at Boyce, Dr. Singleton irradiated a number of seeds with cobalt 60. He plans to continue his work as director of the newly established National Colonial Farm.

At Bryan Point on the Potomac, near Mount Vernon, the farm is dedicated to growing and producing early American crops in a manner similar to that used by colonists. Perhaps it is fitting that one of the old "crops," hopefully, will someday be the American chestnut—even if it is given an atomic age boost.

And so the fine old tree that is gone from an area equal to fourteen thousand square miles still clings to life by a thread. And cheering for it are millions of people who have never seen it and never will. But from the fond words of those who knew it, they realize that it must have been quite a tree. They will see little of the cream-colored male catkins, sometimes ten inches long, which decorate it in July. They'll probably never see the smaller female catkins that develop into those fierce, armored burrs protecting the two or three nuts in their velvet chambers.

Nor will they know the howls of pain that followed a careless step on a new-fallen chestnut burr and put an end to "summer barefoot days," as my mother calls them—days when chestnut trees overhung the road to school.

Yet hope for the chestnut still remains in those plucky sprouts, the rare old patriarchs, the hybrids and grafted trees, and in the "hot" radiation chamber.

Hope, too, arrived in yesterday's mail with a letter from a woman in Short Hills, New Jersey. "We have three beautiful, healthy trees in our yard with a diameter of about nine to ten inches each. We have had a good crop of chestnuts from them every fall."

Advising her to get in touch with her county agricultural agent at once—which is a good place to start if you know of a chestnut more than eight inches in diameter—I sent a letter to the New Jersey Agricultural Experiment Station at Rutgers. I hope to see the trees for myself soon.

If some improvement crew doesn't get there first.

Galls

As a boy I was fascinated with the willow pine-cone gall, an odd growth of plant scales produced by the activities of a tiny, flylike creature known as a midge. A female midge lays eggs on tender willow buds in spring. Each egg turns into a little maggot that, by its secretions, stimulates the gall to develop. Thus the midge, which feeds within the gall tissue obligingly supplied by the plant, is provided with food and shelter, as are a host of other insects and arachnids that quickly move in.

This story is repeated with hundreds of variations every summer and fall, even to the freeloaders, for in addition to *Rhabdophaga strobiloides*, the willow midge, there are several thousand other gall-makers known. Their handiwork is in every garden and weedlot.

Actually, they should be called gall-causers, for nearly always it is the host plant that makes the gall. Whether the little intruder is a midge, wasp, aphid, mite, nematode, fungus, or bacteria, it is the presence of the egg or the substances produced by its growth that triggers the gall process. Many gall organisms can live solely on one plant species. And each organism causes the plant to develop a gall shaped and formed especially for it alone.

On goldenrod, for example, the stem is often swollen into hard little balls. These are galls caused by an attractive spotted-winged fly about the size of a housefly. At the same time, the top of the stem may be compressed into a dense little rosette of leaves, the work of a midge. Somewhere else on the same stem may be an elongated swelling. This is the home of the caterpillar of a tiny moth.

Many gall-makers have strong jaws as larvae, while in the adult stage their mouth parts may be weak or missing. So the larva must prepare early for its eventual escape. It may chew almost completely through the gall tissue, leaving just a thin layer to burst through later, or it may bite all the way through, carefully blocking its escape hatch with a little plug of chewed-up material.

These trap doors and the vulnerable condition of the young gall allow access to uninvited guests. Many feed alongside the rightful occupant. Others, however, are there for a more insidious purpose—destruction of the gall-maker itself.

Galls may be found on any number of plants and trees. The familiar oak apples attached to a leaf, which resemble brown hollowed-out ping-pong balls, show the presence of a tiny wasp larva. Another wasp is responsible for a woolly oak gall somewhat like a fuzzy marble.

Spruces may suffer from the aphid gall, which resembles a prickly, half-formed spruce cone. Little cock's-comb structures on elm leaves are the work of more aphids. Dozens live in each comb. Prize rosebushes may develop massy rose galls, little tufts of coarse brown "cotton." These are caused by a small wasp.

Then there are fungus galls, the unsightly black knots on cherry and plum trees and the round cedar galls that produce orange fingerlike structures during rainy spells. Spores from cedar galls eventually drift to apple trees, where they produce apple rust. So, even though drought may have its ill effects, at least it lessens rust damage to apples.

The Look of Christmas

HE STOOD in the path and faced me with a soundless snarl. The moon, bright on the snow, illumined his white coat and his glittering eyes. Although I held my breath so that its vapor wouldn't cloud my vision, my heart beat so that I could scarcely focus my eyes to see him clearly.

As we poised there, both with one foot lifted for the next step, there was a soft sound in the spruce above me. A stiff branch, holding aloft a puff of snow, had released its hold. The snow cascaded down through the tree in a powdery shower. It sifted down about me, making a whispering curtain that shut out all but itself. And when it finally cleared away, the weasel was gone.

I went back to look at his tracks. He'd been following me as I walked along the path through our woods. Curiosity, no doubt. And when I'd turned and found him loping from one footprint to the next, he'd chosen to depart, perhaps to find something more his own size. This might be a luckless rabbit or a ruffed grouse buried for warmth beneath the insulation of a snowdrift.

My weasel in his winter coat of ermine was just one tiny detail in the great panorama of winter in Vermont. Those snow-laden spruces, of course, were another. So was the moon, which seldom seems brighter than when it is full over a new snow. So too was the stream which gurgled some-where, hidden beneath a crystal blanket with its sound seeming to come from everywhere. And all of them put together added another facet to what might be called the look of Christmas.

Actually, it's more than just a look. Christmas in the Green Mountains, if you're lucky enough to be able to enjoy it at your leisure, involves the other senses, too. It even includes a sixth sense of awareness, whetted to a fine edge as you step softly in the moonlit snow—and whirl to find a fourteen-inch weasel stalking you.

Often our whole family goes on these walks. The sights and sounds and smells of the rest of the year are gone now, but there are others that have taken their place. We've learned that it's a good time to discover the other creatures that are sharing the woods with us.

We follow the trail of a deer as it browses the twigs of a maple and scratches at a ledge for buried ferns and lichens. A dead leaf hanging, twisted, from a twig turns out to be sewn together with silk. It's the cradle of next summer's moth, now hanging in the open as a pupa. It's protected from the bitter Vermont winter not so much by the flimsy leaf as by the very nature of its body fluids. They contain so little water that they're like a thick, unfreezing syrup. But it still may not survive the winter. Birds and white-footed mice, their stomachs pinched by hunger, seek out the tiny bundle of concentrated food.

There are more signs of life. One time my wife and I were climbing a steep incline. Peg slipped and grabbed at an old stump. A great chunk of the bark tore loose and a little shower of sleepers peppered the snow. There were beetles, spiders, flies, and even a drowsy caterpillar. A pungent smell to the wood told us that great black carpenter ants were probably wintering in its pithy center.

A dried goldenrod at the base of the stump sported a swollen gall halfway up its stalk—the winter home of still more life. Inside would be a rice-sized white grub of the goldenrod gall fly, tucked inside the spongy walls of its home. And often if we cut the gall open, we find that the grub in turn has become the winter home of still other creatures, tiny wasps which utilize the tissues of their unwilling host to tide them over until spring.

Sometime in early December our walks take on a new meaning. "Time to get the Christmas tree," announces one of the children. So we take the ax and start off for the woods. We've picked the tree out earlier, for it's hard to be sure of its shape when the branches are laden with snow.

Tom and Roger like the aroma of balsam fir, while Janice and Alison like the luxurious thick branches of spruce. My own preference is for hemlock, the tree most easily obtained during my Connecticut boyhood. Peg goes along with the children and myself with happy impartiality. "We'll love our tree no matter what it is," she says.

Although most Vermont evergreens may appear similar, it's easy to pick out the differences among the types of Christmas trees. If the northwoods aroma of the balsam doesn't identify it for you, just pull off a needle or two. If it's balsam, the needle leaves a flat, round scar. Those of other trees leave a short little stub. Balsam needles are rounded on the ends, too, so you can decorate the tree without discomfort.

Not so with the spruces. When we bring in a spruce, those sharp, four-sided needles stick out stiffly from all sides of the branches, so that we're in danger of getting impaled as we trim the tree. But it's often worth the trouble. Spruces are wonderfully thick, with needles all along the branches and with pendant twigs.

Usually, when we get a spruce, it's a red spruce, with orange-reddish twigs and a warm yellowish hint to the foliage. One year I brought in a tree which had a whitish tinge. It was a spruce, all right, but when a friend of mine got a look at it, he burst out laughing.

"What on earth ails you?" I demanded.

"You'll see," he grinned.

In a few days, I understood. My spruce still looked good, but it was developing a certain air. Reminded us of the time our dog chased a skunk under the lilac bush.

Peg looked at the tree as if she expected it to burst into flames. "Good heavens! What kind of a spruce did he say it was?"

"He didn't say," I told her. "I've always known it as white spruce. But I never had one in the house before."

And I've never had one since. The name white spruce may be a perfect fit, but so is the name my friend confessed sometime later: skunk spruce.

My favorite Christmas tree, the hemlock, is unmistakable. It's our only common conifer which lacks a stiff terminal spire. Instead, its tip droops gracefully, as do all its lesser limbs and twigs. It looks as if it's already decorated with green tinsel icicles. Its twigs lack any buds at the tip, thus differing from firs and spruces. And flat little hemlock needles, borne in a flat spray, are soft and rounded or notched at the tips.

The remaining Christmas tree is, like many residents of our Green Mountain State, a relative newcomer. Scotch pine, unknown to many, is first choice for others. Planted by the thousands here in Vermont and in many parts of the country, it has become America's leading Christmas tree. Its flattened, twisted needles spring in twos from a little sheath. Like balsam fir, it's wonderful at holding its foliage for weeks in the house.

Although our trip to the woods for a yuletide tree has become a family tradition, it's by no means the only time we all get to enjoy the look of Christmas. There are at least two other occasions.

One of these, oddly enough, is during the bitterest weather, when the sky is clearest. While the temperature plummets until the maples in the woods snap like a pistol shot with the cold, we bundle up for a look at the stars. Our breath crystallizes with a soft hiss as it meets the air. Above us, the time-less story of the hunt hangs suspended in the sky.

High in the southeast is the winter constellation of Orion, the mighty hunter. He stands poised, ready to hurl a lethal blow across the black gulf at the Great Bear, which we also know as the Big Dipper. His belt and diagonal sword makes a great square letter "Q" in the sky. At his side, farther east, leaps his faithful dog, Canis Major, bearing in his mouth the brightest object outside of our own solar system—Sirius, the Dog Star, only 8.8 light-years away. As we contemplate the glitter of Sirius, we think of that other star in the east, twenty centuries back in time.

Almost overhead the little cluster of the Pleiades stands aloof in its own family group. We call it the Seven Sisters; the Indians used to test their vision by trying to count all seven stars. My eyes get watery after number six. And a bit to the north sits the queen of the heavens, Cassiopeia, in her W-shaped chair.

With our faces tingling from the cold, we pick out an entire zoo in the sky. Up there, the ancients identified a swan, bull, hare, lynx, lion, dragon, and, as if overwhelmed with the immensity of it all, Cetus the Whale. Somewhere, too, according to Indian legend, waits the courageous animal known as the fisher, gathering strength for his heroic rush to the upper sky. There, summoning all his daring, he will tear a hole in the heavens and let the summer down to earth once more.

We take still another family outing on a December night. Oddly enough, it may be heralded by an electronic gadget on our shelf. "What's the matter with the radio tonight?" Peg wonders, as the Burlington station begins to sound as if it's having an outsized fish-fry. We twist the dial for better tuning, but to no avail. Burlington, thirty miles away, may fade completely. Then, searching further on the dial, we pick up Hartford, Connecticut, two hundred miles distant—or perhaps even that clear-channel companion of listeners all over America, WWVA in Wheeling, West Virginia.

Suddenly one of us realizes what is happening. "Northern lights!" we cry and rush out to view the spectacle. Often it's just a false alarm, but since the aurora borealis may be triggered by the same electrical disturbance that upsets our radio, it's always worth the effort to see if the lights are playing overhead.

As we in Vermont gaze at the glowing curtains that wave in the sky, or view the luminous shafts which shoot up toward the zenith, it's hard to realize that the display above us originated some ninety million miles away. The sun's electrical storms and sunspots, many of them larger than our entire earth, send waves of energy surging into space. A smattering of this energy is caught by gases in our upper atmosphere. The gases glow and flicker like the gas in a fluorescent light—and there's our aurora borealis.

One winter evening a friend of mine was entertaining some visitors from New York City. They regaled him with stories of the Great White Way, the glitter of Times Square, and the excitement of the theater district. The tales would have continued but for young Philip's discovery that the northern lights were playing in the sky outside. So the guests dutifully followed him out into the yard.

They stood in awe as the spectacle unfolded some three hundred miles overhead. Finally, one of the visitors found his voice. "Why," he said, "that's magnificent!"

"Yep," admitted his host, "it ain't bad—for Vermont."

There's one other display that's not bad, either. And, to give full dimension to the look of Christmas, it must be mentioned here, even though it may cause a few second thoughts about frozen winter in a chilly land. This is the annual event known simply as The Thaw.

Our thaw may occur at any time, give or take a couple of weeks, around the Christmas season. But it somehow always manages to happen. As one of my old-timer neighbors tells me, "I've seen a thousand winters and never seen one without a thaw yet."

At some point the cold, which has been clutching the countryside tightly, releases its hold. Perhaps it's just to get a better grip or maybe it relents a bit. At any rate, the weather changes. And while people all over America swap nostalgic Christmas cards with deep-snow Vermont scenes on them, the people who live right in those Christmas cards listen to the soft sound of rain as it thuds into that snow. They watch rivulets form in the meadows and pastures, trickling down to the brooks and streams.

If the warm spell lasts more than a day or so, the streams begin to swell. Their ceiling of ice becomes a partition between two rivers, one flowing above it and one hidden beneath. We stand on the bridge in front of our house and listen to the ice groan and crack as it strives to regain the position where normal ice should be—on top of the water.

Finally a great slab breaks loose. Ponderously it rises to the surface. Its going weakens the other ice about it and more chunks follow.

Then, suddenly, as if at a signal, the ice of the whole river is in motion. Grinding, rumbling, it tumbles downstream. Urged on by the pressure of the swollen waters, it rushes forward. Small trees along the stream disappear under the juggernaut. Our house, some fifty feet from the flood, feels the impact of great chunks as they crash and stop momentarily against the boulders of the stream bed.

But even as the river scours itself clean, the cold begins to return. Within a few hours the water is back in its banks and that slushy snow has crystallized to where it will support the weight of a man, or even a car. The temperature, which may have been sixty at noon, is down around zero by midnight.

Now, with the normal Vermont winter here again, we settle back to our daily rounds. We put out suet and seeds for the bluejays, chickadees, nuthatches, and woodpeckers. We listen for the whistle of the strengthening wind and the distant hoot of an owl on the slopes of Mt. Abraham, some three miles from our home. The smell of snow is brought to us and the first few crystals sting our faces.

Soon the land is white again. The sound of the repentant river fades to a murmur under its new coating of ice. The skunk, raccoon, and woodchuck, perhaps wakened by the unusual warmth or a trickle of icewater into the den, go back to their slumbers. My weasel, which may have found a few insomniac insects during the thaw, returns to rabbits and mice.

And pervading it all is that which millions of Americans somehow understand and for which they are glad, even though they may never set foot in our Green Mountain State: the look of a Vermont Christmas.